D1417782

IMMORTALS
of the
SCREEN

IMMORTALS
of the
SCREEN

Compiled by
RAY STUART

Book design by Czeslaw Z. Banasiewicz

BONANZA BOOKS · NEW YORK

Table of Contents

JEAN HARLOW

Born: March 3, 1911, Kansas City, Missouri. Died: 1937.

Height: 5', 3½". Weight: 109 lbs. Blonde hair and gray-blue eyes. She spent the first ten years of her life in a suburban home outside Kansas City. She attended private kindergarten and the Barstow school for girls. When she was sixteen, she ran away and was married. She went to California on her honeymoon and decided to stay, and Jean's parents moved to California to be near their only daughter.

Sheer chance or fate brought Jean into pictures. One day she went to Fox Studios with a girlfriend who was working in pictures. While waiting for her friend, she was seen by one of the Fox officials, who gave her a letter to the casting director. On the advice of the casting director she registered at the central casting office, and after a few days' work, Hal Roach offered her a part in one of his comedies. She played in two-reelers at the Roach Studio. After an eight-month interval, she tried her luck once more and was given a second lead in a Christie picture. At the Christie Studio, she met Ben Lyon and James Hall, who were making "Hell's Angels." They took her to the Caddo Studio for a test and introduced her to Howard Hughes. The result was the playing of the feminine lead in "Hell's Angels" and the beginning of a platinum blonde craze.

Her screen credits include: *Hell's Angels, The Secret Six, The Iron Man, The Public Enemy, Goldie, Platinum Blonde, Three Wise Girls, Beast Of The City, Red-Headed Woman, Red Dust, Hold Your Man, Dinner At Eight, Blonde Bombshell, The Girl From Missouri, Reckless, China Seas, Riff Raff.* Her latter pictures were: *Wife Vs. Secretary,* with Clark Gable and Myrna Loy; *Suzy* with Franchot Tone and Cary Grant; *Libeled Lady* with William Powell, Myrna Loy, Spencer Tracy; *Personal Property* with Robert Taylor; and *Saratoga* with Clark Gable and Lionel Barrymore.

Her untimely death in 1937 was a great shock and a terrible loss to her many, many fans all over the world.

Her six years under contract to M.G.M. were ones of great fulfillment and smashing box-office successes, but she will always be remembered as the little platinum blonde who skyrocketed to success in *Hell's Angels.*

JEAN HARLOW

Untitled Hal Roach Comedy
Circa 1928

In this comedy she played a small part. In this scene we see her working with Bryant Washburn, a famous actor dating back from the days of Essanay Films in Chicago. She played several parts and bits on the Hal Roach lot before her big chance came. She also worked with Stan Laurel and Oliver Hardy and proved a very good foil for their zany antics.

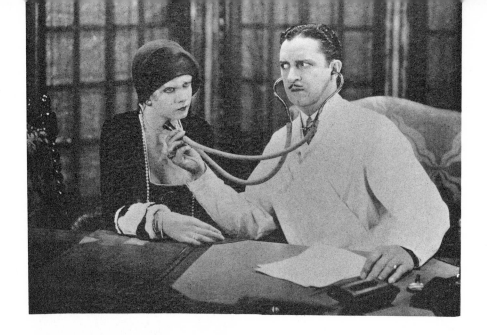

Hell's Angels
(United Artists, 1930).

Howard Hughes was about to make this big aviation spectacular with Ben Lyon and James Hall as the young aviator leads. When he was shown Jean Harlow's test film, he immediately engaged her for the feminine lead in the picture. This aviation story of World War I, with Jean Harlow providing the love interest, made her a topflight star, and it was not long after that she was placed under contract to M.G.M. Studios.

Dinner At Eight
(M.G.M., 1933).

This picture was one of the spectaculars of 1933, and to all intents and purposes practically every player on the M.G.M. lot was in the cast which included Jean Harlow, Wallace Beery, John Barrymore, Lionel Barrymore, Marie Dressler, Billie Burke, Madge Evans and Lee Tracy.

Personal Property, (M.G.M., 1937).

In her years at M.G.M. she was to costar with all the great personalities and topflight stars of the screen. In this picture she costarred with Robert Taylor and Reginald Owen. Her other contemporaries were: Clark Gable, Spencer Tracy, Lee Tracy, Franchot Tone, Cary Grant, Frank Morgan, Lionel Barrymore, Lewis Stone.

Saratoga, (M.G.M., 1937).

In this horse-racing story of Saratoga Race Track, Clark Gable played the part of a professional gambler. Jean Harlow played horse-owner Lionel Barrymore's daughter. Their meeting and romance created an M.G.M. top quality film. Jean Harlow died before the completion of this picture, and M.G.M. was forced to use a double to finish the film.

RUDOLPH VALENTINO

Born May 10, 1895, died 1926. Birthplace — Castellaneta, Italy. Height 5'11". Weight 156 lbs. Black hair and brown eyes. His mother was French and his father was a captain in the Italian cavalry. His early schooling was in a military academy and finally the Royal Academy of Agriculture. At the age of eighteen he arrived in New York City in the year of 1913 and after several jobs he drifted into the cafe of New York. It was the height of the tango craze. He was hired by an Exhibition dancer, Bonny Glass, as a dance partner. They played Rectors, the Palace, The Winter Garden and many cafes.

Bonny Glass retiring, Valentino took on a new partner by the name of Joan Sawyer. He was in the musical comedy called the *Masked Model* when he landed in California and became friendly with Norman Kerry who encouraged him to try the movies. Nothing came of it and he was forced to dance in cafes again for his living.

Valentino spent the time from 1917-20 working in some sixteen films playing bits and very small roles and suddenly he was called back to Metro. The great writer June Mathis had seen him work in a small role in *The Eyes Of Youth* and she was instrumental in securing for him the part of Julio in *The Four Horsemen Of The Apocalypse*. This picture was directed and produced by Rex Ingram one of the greatest craftsman of his time. This film became one of the greatest box office smashes of all time.

From his success in *The Four Horsemen* he became the biggest box office draw in the country and went on into other successes in his short lived career. His star screen credits include: *Camille*, Metro 1921; *The Conquering Power*, Metro 1921; *The Sheik*, Paramount 1921; *Beyond The Rocks*, Paramount 1922; *Blood And Sand*, 1922; *Young Rajah*, 1922; *Monsieur Beaucaire*, 1924; *A Sainted Devil*, 1924; *Cobra*, 1925; *The Eagle*, United Artists 1925. His last film was *Son of the Sheik*, United Artists 1926.

At the height and pinnacle of his success in the year of 1926 Valentino was in New York City making public appearances for augmented publicity in *The Son Of The Sheik*, when he was seized with a gall stone attack. He was taken to The Polyclinic Hospital and after an operation died from peritonitis. While his work as Julio, The Argentinian, Tango Dancer and Libertine, who died on the battle field fighting for his father's country forever immortalized him, he will always be remembered as *The Sheik* in the picture of that name.

The Four Horsemen Of The Apocalypse, (Metro, 1921). Rudolph Valentino was costarred with Alice Terry, Joseph Swickard, John Saintpolis and Alan Hale.

The Sheik, (Paramount, 1921).
This plot was adapted from Hull's great novel and costarred Agnes Ayres and Valentino. It was the first picture Valentino did for Paramount. George Melford directed this picture.

Camille, (Metro, 1921).
This famous old stage classic combined Nazimova's whimsically strange version and Natacha Rambova's colorful settings with Valentino playing the role of Armand.

The Son Of The Sheik,
(United Artists, 1926).
George Fitzmaurice directed this picture. In response to popular demand United Artists revived and modernized this new version of *The Sheik*. Rudolph Valentino enacted a dual role of the aged Sheik and also that of his son. Vilma Banky had the romantic female lead and Agnes Ayres also played her part in the picture. This was Valentino's last picture.

Blood and Sand, (Paramount, 1922).
In this story of the Spanish bull fighter, Valentino is considered to have given one of his best performances. In this Ibanez novel the story portrayed a conceited toreador whose fortunes ebb and whose public and followers vilify him. This picture was directed by Fred Niblo.

ROSS ALEXANDER

ROSS ALEXANDER

Ross Alexander gained his greatest screen fame with the Warner Brothers Studio. Among his screen credits are: *Flirtation Walk, Gentlemen Are Born, Maybe It's Love, A Midsummer Night's Dream, Crashing Society, We're In The Money, Shipmates Forever* and *Captain Blood.*

Born in New York City, the son of a New York leather merchant, he gained a high school education. When he was 16 years old Blanche Yurka gave him his first chance in legitimate theater in *Enter Madame.*

This auspicious beginning was followed by a succession of good roles in such plays as: *That's Gratitude, The Stork Is Dead, Honeymoon, No Questions Asked, The Party's Over* and *Let's Be Gay.*

His own native ability was sharpened and improved by playing in the same cast with such experienced troupers as Philip Merivale, Francine Larrimore, Frank Craven, Donald Meek, Kathryn Alexander, George Barbier and Alan Dinehart. He had his share of stock company experience in Boston, Mass. and Louisville, Kentucky.

Ross Alexander and Patricia Ellis costarred to create *Boulder Dam,* a Warner Bros. Production, 1936.

In *Applesauce*, a Warner Bros. comedy, Ross Alexander and Anita Louise were costarred for the first time.

In *Ready, Willing And Able*, (Warner Bros.), Winifred Shaw costarred with Ross Alexander in one of their famous comedies.

In *Captain Blood*, Rafael Sabatini's great pirate novel, (the Warner Bros. production), we see Ross Alexander in the rigging of a pirate ship as he portrays his supporting role to Errol Flynn's "Captain Blood."

In this scene from Warner Bros.' *A Midsummer Night's Dream* we see Jean Muir and Ross Alexander.

ROSCOE FATTY ARBUCKLE

Born: Smith Center, Kansas, March 24, 1887. Height 5′, 10″. Weight: 245 lbs.
Light Hair, Blue Eyes. Education: Grammar School, Santa Clara, Calif.

He was an illustrated song singer, vaudeville, carnival, burlesque, musical
comedy and comic opera star. He entered the theater in 1900 and worked for
Selig Poli scope   Company (1907), Mack Sennett Keystone Comedies from
1913-17. He entered into partnership with Joseph Schenck and produced two
reelers independently. From 1919-21 he was under contract to Famous Players
appearing in the following films: *The Roundup, Life Of The Party, Dollar
A Year Man, A Traveling Salesman, Gasoline Gus,* and *Brewsters Millions.*

Fatty Arbuckle and Minta Durfee in an early Mack Sennett Keystone Comedy. Arbuckle costarred also in many of these Keystone Comedies with Mabel Normand, Harriet Hammond, Marie Prevost, Phyliss Haver and others.

The Roundup, (Famous Players-Lasky, 1920). In this early comedy Eddy Sutherland played a romantic cowboy lead. He was to become one of the greatest directors to work for Famous Players.

Roscoe Fatty Arbuckle in a comedy made at Fort Lee in 1916. At Fatty Arbuckle's table is Minta Durfee, his first wife. Jack Pollard is about to receive the siphoned tribute of the comedian.

Traveling Salesman, (Famous Players-Lasky, 1921). In this photo Charles Ogle and William V. Mong, two of the great character actors on the Paramount roster, supported Fatty Arbuckle.

Gasoline Gus, (Famous Players-Lasky, 1921). In this film Fatty Arbuckle was costarred with Lila Lee. During the time he worked for Famous Players he was at the height of his powers and his fame. The scandal that was to prevent the fulfillment of his career also led to his untimely death.

RENEE ADOREE

Born: Lille, France. Died: October, 1933. Height: 5'1". Weight: 117 lbs. Blue eyes and brown hair.

Her film credits are: *La Boheme, Tin Gods, Blarney, The Exquisite Sinner, The Flaming Forest, Mr. Wu, The Cossacks, The Pagan, Tide Of Empire, Forbidden Hours.*

She is immortalized for her role of "Melisande" in *The Big Parade*, playing the feminine lead opposite John Gilbert, together with Karl Dane, as "Swede."

RENEE ADOREE

Renee Adoree and Polly Moran, the great comedienne, in an early M.G.M. picture.

In *Big Parade* we see John Gilbert back from the war in the final scene as he and Renee Adoree as "Melisande" meet. This picture made stars of John Gilbert, Renee Adoree and Karl Dane.

In Tolstoy's *Redemption* we see Renee Adoree as Masha, the gypsy singing girl, costarred with John Gilbert. This film was produced by M.G.M. in 1929.

Any plot written by Elinor Glyn was bound to be sexy. In *Man And Maid* (M.G.M., 1925), Renee Adoree is seen in one of the most provocative roles of her great career.

Mr. Wu, (M.G.M., 1927).
Renee Adoree costarred with Ralph Forbes and Lon Chaney. In a moment of levity off the set, Ralph Forbes, Mira Adoree and Renee Adoree demonstrate Chinese jazz.

19

GEORGE ARLISS

GEORGE ARLISS

Born: London, England, April 10, 1868. His stage career started very young; he entered the legitimate theater in a play with Mrs. Patrick Campbell.

After a distinguished stage career he went on to his greatest success, *Disraeli*. Warner Bros. contracted with him and he gained fame in *Disraeli*, 1929; *The Green Goddess*, 1930; *Old English*, 1931; *Man Who Played God; The Millionaire; Alexander Hamilton*, 1932, and *A Successful Calamity*. Leaving the Warner Bros. banner he did *A King's Vacation, The Working Man* and *Voltaire*, and in 1934: *The House of Rothschild, The Lost Gentlemen;* in 1935: *Iron Duke*, an English G.B. picture. Following this picture he portrayed the title role of *Cardinal Richelieu*. In England he once more worked for G.B. Studios and finished *Mr. Hobo* and *East Meets West*.

He will forever be immortalized for his film characterization of *"Disraeli."*

In London, England, 1930, George Arliss plays the part of an Eastern potentate who meets a Saxon girl with resulting romantic complication. In this scene he is costarred with Lucie Mannheim.

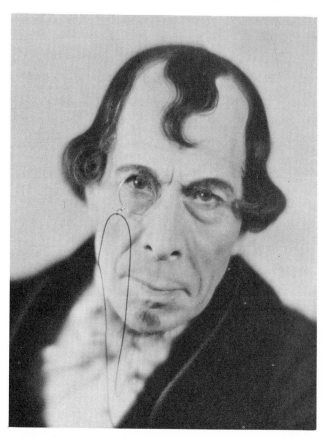

For many years George Arliss played *Disraeli* on the English and American stages so well and so competently that when the time came for him to do this role for the Warner Bros. film it was only natural that it should immortalize him.

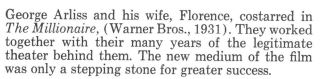
George Arliss and his wife, Florence, costarred in *The Millionaire*, (Warner Bros., 1931). They worked together with their many years of the legitimate theater behind them. The new medium of the film was only a stepping stone for greater success.

Cardinal Richelieu, (United Artists, 1935). In this scene we see him play the title role with Edward Arnold as King Louis.

In the year of 1933, Mr. Arliss played the great French philosopher Voltaire in the Warner Bros. film of that title.

21

HENRY ARMETTA

One of the greatest Italian comedians of the American screen was born at Palermo, Italy, July 4, 1888, one of seven children born to John and Rosalie Armetta. After his education in Palermo public schools, Armetta, an adventurous youth, made his way aboard a ship at the age of fourteen, a stowaway discovered when the ship docked in Boston.

The youthful Armetta was turned over to the police by ship authorities. They found a man who guaranteed to give the boy a home and work if the police would release him. This man was John Armato, a barber, and within a few days Henry found himself lathering customers preparatory to their being shaved by Armato. After a few months Armetta found work in a barber shop in the Lambs' Club in New York. Here Armetta aided the barbers and also became a pants presser.

During his second year in this shop Raymond Hitchcock, attracted by young Armetta's eagerness to please and his jovial disposition, offered the pants presser a small part in his production of *Yankee Consul.*

After many years in legitimate theater Armetta landed a part in the *Littlest Rebel* starring Mary Miles Minter. For months thereafter Armetta worked at the Fox East Coast Studios.

Henry Armetta came to Hollywood in 1923. As an Italian character comedian his services were in great demand in Hollywood and among his screen credits are: *Seventh Heaven, Street Angel, Lady Of The Pavement, In Old Arizona, Cat And The Fiddle, Farewell To Arms* and others.

HENRY ARMETTA

Top Of The Town, (Universal Film Production). In this musical film Henry Armetta played a featured supporting role to Doris Nolan and George Murphy. In this scene we see him at the helm of a camera truck taking Carolyn Mason, Juanita Field and Mary Daair for a ride. Henry Armetta worked in many Universal Films, playing both comedy and drama.

Night Life Of The Gods,
(Universal Studio Production, 1935).
This comedy-fantasy brought forth some of the weirdest, way out, characterizations that were ever conceived on any set at the Universal Studios.

Road Demon, A Sports Adventure Film
(20th Century-Fox Production, 1938).
Henry Armetta was now working for all the major film studios. Here Henry Armetta and Joan Valerie are seen in a spirited discussion.

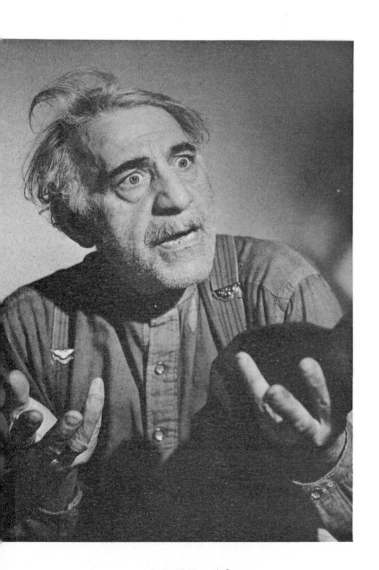

Winner Takes All, (20th Century-Fox Production, 1939).
In this scene we see Henry Armetta with some of his contemporaries of the Thirties. From left to right, top row: Slim Summerville, Henry Armetta, Kane Richmond. Bottom row: Gloria Stuart and Tony Martin.

A Bell For Adano,
(20th Century-Fox Production, 1945).
This film starred John Hodiak and Gene Tierney. It was a Second World War story with heavy religious overtones. The locale was Italy. The screen-play was adapted from author John Hersey's best seller.

EDWARD ARNOLD

Born: New York City, February 18, 1890. Stage experience in the *Jazz Singer*, *The Nervous Wreck*, *The Third Little Show*, *Whistling In The Dark* and others.

With this experience behind him he came to Hollywood. His screen credits are: *Rasputin And The Empress*, M.G.M.; *The White Sister*, *Whistling In The Dark*, and *Man Of The Nile*, M.G.M.

He was teamed with Mae West in *I'm No Angel*, Paramount. From there he went on to greater success. Some of his roles have immortalized him upon the American screen. I refer to *Crime And Punishment*, Columbia; *You Can't Take It With You*, Columbia. He will always be remembered as "Diamond Jim Brady."

EDWARD ARNOLD

You Can't Take It With You, (Columbia Film Production, 1938).

This picture is considered to be one of the greatest and inspired productions ever produced by Frank Capra. Edward Arnold had some of the greatest players of the era with him including James Stewart, Jean Arthur, and Lionel Barrymore. Edward Arnold's work in this film opened the eyes of the studio heads and made them realize the true scope of his acting.

Lillian Russell
(20th Century-Fox Production, 1940).
In this film Alice Faye played the title role of Lillian Russell and Edward Arnold played Diamond Jim Brady. According to legend the real Diamond Jim Brady was the originator of the high pressure selling system. The present method of wining and dining the potential buyer is supposed to have started with Diamond Jim Brady's departure from orthodox methods of selling.

Unholy Partners, (M.G.M. Film Production, 1941).
Edward Arnold was teamed with Edward G. Robinson, and Loraine Day furnished the love interest. The locale was New York; the men were bitter enemies and Loraine Day was Robinson's aide in a newspaper office.

Kismet, (M.G.M. Production, 1944).
This film starred Ronald Colman as a beggar-magician who masquerades as a prince. In this scene Edward Arnold plays the grand vizier. Seated alongside of him is Marlene Dietrich who plays the queen of his harem. The supporting cast included James Craig, Joy Ann Page, Hugh Herbert, Hobart Cavanaugh, Harry Davenport, Robert Warwick and Florence Bates.

The Youngest Profession,
(M.G.M. Film Production, 1943).
In this humorous tale of teen-age, movie-mad young-sters Virginia Weidler and Jean Porter were cast as America's most ardent autograph addicts. The sup-porting cast included Edward Arnold, Marta Linden, John Carroll, Ann Ayars and Dick Simmons. Prac-tically every star under contract on the M.G.M. lot made cameo appearances in this picture, including Greer Garson, Walter Pidgeon, Robert Taylor and William Powell.

GRACIE ALLEN

Born: July 26, 1902, San Francisco, California. The team of Burns and Allen delighted national radio audiences for better than 17 years. Their motion picture debut was in *International House*.

Her screen credits are: *Big Broadcast of 1936, Love In Bloom, College Swing, Honolulu, Gracie Allen Murder Case, Mr. & Mrs. North*, and *Two Girls And A Sailor*. The zany, rollicking domestic comedy of George and Gracie will never be forgotten. She will be remembered by millions of admirers in her family comedies as "Our Gracie."

In 1936 Paramount teamed Jack Benny, George Burns and Gracie Allen, Martha Raye, and that famous comedienne Mary Boland to create one of their most famous comedies, *College Holiday*.

The year is 1937, the studio is R.K.O. and the title of the film, *A Damsel In Distress*. Gracie and George seem out of sorts!

College Swing, (Paramount, 1938).
George Burns and Gracie Allen did their usual rollicking comedy to great effect with practically everybody on the Paramount lot including Martha Raye, Bob Hope, Ben Blue and Betty Grable.

S. S. Van Dine wrote *The Gracie Allen Murder Case*, Paramount produced it and Warren William, Ellen Drew, Kent Taylor, and Donald MacBride supported Gracie in her zany-pseudo horror picture. The year was 1939.

27

LIONEL ATWILL

Born: March 1, 1885, Croydon, England. Height: 5'10½". Weight: 172 lbs. Dark brown hair, grey eyes. Educated at Mercers' School in London.

He made his stage debut in 1904, appearing in *The Walls Of Jericho*, *The Little Minister*, *Hedda Gabler*, etc. His screen credits include: *Silent Witness*, Fox, 1932; *Mystery Of The Wax Museum*, Warner Bros., 1932; *The Sphinx*, Monogram Studios, 1933; *Song Of Songs*, Paramount, 1933; *The Solitaire Man*, M.G.M., 1933; *Secret Of The Blue Room*, Universal, 1933; *The Devil Is A Woman*, Paramount, 1936, and *Mark Of The Vampire*, one of the early horror films.

Lionel Atwill became a master actor of the macabre and as a result devoted much of the latter stages of his career to the weird, the ghastly, the morbid and the supernatural.

LIONEL ATWILL

Lady Of Secrets, (Columbia, 1936). In this picture he was co-starred with Ruth Chatterton. They were ably supported by Otto Kruger, Marian Marsh and Lloyd Nolan.

28

One of Lionel Atwill's greatest hobbies was attending murder trials. This undoubtedly led to his masterly portrayals in horror pictures. This macabre horror scene shows Atwill in morbid contemplation of a cadaver, probably deciding the ultimate disposal of this charming corpse.

Charlie Chan In Panama, (Fox, 1940).
Sidney Toler in his character, Charlie Chan, had Lionel Atwill and Jean Rogers as costars. Warner Oland was the first Charlie Chan in the early Thirties. Sidney Toler was the 2nd Charlie Chan, and after him came Roland Winters.

The Ghost Of Frankenstein,
(Universal, 1942).
In this interpretation of Frankenstein, Lon Chaney, Jr. played the title role with Lionel Atwill and Sir Cedric Hardwicke lending support. In the course of time the studio used different actors for the part of Frankenstein, in addition to Lon Chaney, Jr., Glenn Strange acted in several versions and Bela Lugosi, that old master of horror, did his interpretation of Frankenstein.

The House Of Frankenstein, (Universal, 1944).

MISCHA AUER

Birthplace: St. Petersburg, Russia, November 17, 1905. Height: 6'2". Weight: 165 lbs. Dark hair and brown eyes.

His stage credits are: *The Magda, The Wild Duck, The Riddle Woman* and *The Kibitzer*. He entered pictures in 1928. In the early part of his career he played sinister heavies; in later years he proved that he had a definite flair for comedy and accordingly became one of the screens leading comedians. His supporting roles gave meaning and significance to many productions such as: *My Man Godfrey, The Gay Desperado, Three Smart Girls, Lives Of A Bengal Lancer, Clive Of India* and *The Princess Comes Across.*

MISCHA AUER

The Rage Of Paris, (A Universal Production, 1938).

The feminine lead was Danielle Darrieux, the famous French actress. Costarred with her were Mischa Auer and Douglas Fairbanks Jr.

This picture was a light, rollicking comedy made to order for Mischa Auer's zany comedy talents.

Winterset, (An R.K.O. Radio Picture, 1936).
This film was one of the greatest smash hits ever made by R.K.O. Among a great company of his contemporaries Mischa Auer distinguished himself with a fine performance.

East Side Of Heaven,
(Universal Production, 1939).
In this scene Mischa Auer is the conscience stricken dolt with Bing Crosby as his stern accuser. They were ably supported by Joan Blondell in the leading feminine role. Unquestionably the smoothness and polish of his great performances stemmed from his New York stage career.

Unexpected Father,
(A Universal Production, 1939).
Mischa Auer plays a Greek, and in this photo we see him doing a dance with some of the Universal lovelies. He was under contract to Universal co-starring and performing supporting leads in many of their productions.

Sing Another Chorus,
(Universal Production, 1941).
In this musical Jane Frazee and Sunny O'Dea played the feminine leads, supplied dancing and some of the singing along with Mischa Auer.

GEORGE BANCROFT

Born: September, 1882, Philadelphia, Penn. Died: 1956. Height: 6'2". Weight: 195 lbs. Brown hair, brown eyes. Education: Tomes Institute and United States Naval Academy. Upon leaving school he went to New York and became very successful on the New York stage.

His stage credits include: *The Trail Of The Lonesome Pine, Paid In Full, Old Bill, Cinders,* and others. His first picture for Paramount, *Code Of The West,* brought him to the attention of James Cruze who was casting for *The Pony Express.* He was put under contract to Paramount and some of his great successes with this studio were *The Show Down, The Dragnet, Docks of New York, Wolf of Wall Street, The Mighty Thunder Blow, Ladies Love Brutes, Paramount On Parade, Lady And Gent* and *The World And The Flesh.* In the year of 1933 he starred in *Blood Money* for United Artists.

His hobby was outdoor sports. His virile portrayals of he-men who are able to overcome and control every situation whether it be love, occupation or politics, began a success pattern in George Bancroft's film career. For his exceptionally fine portrayals of the rampant male we can place him among the famous immortals of the screen.

GEORGE BANCROFT

Old Iron Sides,
(Paramount, 1926).
Produced and directed by James Cruze. This picture was one of the big spectaculars of 1926 and nearly everybody under contract at Paramount worked in it. Esther Ralston played one of the big feminine leads and George Bancroft played a fighting sailor aboard the Constitution.

The World And The Flesh,
(Paramount, 1932).
He costarred with Miriam Hopkins who was also under contract to Paramount. This film concerned the Russian revolution with Bancroft playing the part of a Russian seaman and Miriam Hopkins depicting a woman of the Russian nobility.

The Showdown, (Paramount, 1940).
George Bancroft was costarred with Helene Lynch, Leslie Fenton and one of the greatest heavies of the motion pictures, Fred Kohler.

Derelict, (Paramount, 1930).
In the great film drama of the sea Bancroft played one of his mightiest roles. His many film successes embraced the years from 1926-40.

Ladies Love Brutes, (Paramount 1936).
This film was about the construction industry and building of the great sky scrapers in New York. In this photo we see Stanley Fields playing his usual part of the "heavy" with George Bancroft. Bancroft ran the entire gamut of tough occupations such as: building bridges, building sky scrapers, and digging a tunnel under the East River.

33

JOHN BARRYMORE

JOHN BARRYMORE

Born: February 15, 1882, Philadelphia, Penn. His father was Maurice Barrymore and his mother was Georgia Drew.

His stage career started in 1903 and his stage credits include: *Magda, The Affairs Of Anatol, The Yellow Ticket, Peter Ibbetson, The Jest, Richard III*, etc.

His screen credits were: *Raffles, Sherlock Holmes, The Lotus Eaters, Dr. Jekyll And Mr. Hyde, Beau Brummel, The Sea Beast, Don Juan, General Crack, Moby Dick, Arsene Lupin, The Mad Genius, Grand Hotel, Rasputin And The Empress, Reunion In Vienna, Topaze, Dinner At Eight, Counsellor-At-Law, 20th Century* and others.

His father and his mother were classed as the greatest actor and actress of their era, and his brother, Lionel, and also his sister, Ethel, became the most popular theatrical figures of their time. They were affectionately dubbed "The Royal Family of Broadway." He will always be remembered and will eternally typify the role of Francois Villon in *Beloved Rogue*.

The Sea Beast, (Warner Bros. Production, 1926).

Millard Web directed this picture. While the sea action was dramatic his viewing audience will always remember the torrid love scenes with his leading woman, Dolores Costello, who was destined to become his third wife.

Beloved Rogue, (United Artists, 1927).
Allan Crosland directed. Conrad Veidt, the superb German actor played the part of Louis XI. Barrymore's companions were well played by Slim Summerville and Mack Swain, the two great comedians of the old Mack Sennett comedy days.

Rasputin and the Empress, (M.G.M., 1932).
Lionel Barrymore played the part of Rasputin, Ethel Barrymore portrayed the Empress and John Barrymore played the Russian prince. A terrific supporting cast included Ralph Morgan and Edward Arnold.

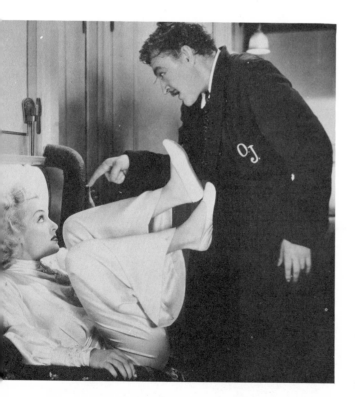

20th Century, (Columbia Picture Corp., 1934).
John Barrymore was costarred with the immortal Carole Lombard. Walter Connolly and Roscoe Karns were in the supporting cast. The picture was directed and produced by Howard Hawks. This theatrical satire was to give Barrymore a chance to be in his own element. The antics and comic situations of a producer and a great actress on board a trans-continental train created a delightful comedy.

Romeo and Juliet, (M.G.M., 1936).
George Cukor, that very fine veteran director, produced this picture. Norma Shearer starred as Juliet and Leslie Howard portrayed the immortal part of Romeo. John Barrymore did an inspired Mercutio. This picture was one of the spectaculars of the M.G.M. studios and several big stars in their own right willingly played supporting roles. Among these were Ralph Forbes and Basil Rathbone.

THEDA BARA

THEDA BARA

Born: 1890. Died: 1955. Birthplace: Cincinnati, Ohio. Height: 5′6″. Weight: 135 lbs. Dark hair and brown eyes. Her real name was Theodosia Goodman.

She had a very brief stage career and then came to Hollywood to try her luck in the motion pictures. Like hundreds of others she haunted studios, waylaid directors and persisted in her quest until she finally was given a very small part in a photo play. But her first real part was the role of the vampire in *A Fool There Was*. A new character had been born in the cinema, the feminine "vamp" which brought Theda Bara to fame. William Fox immediately signed Miss Bara as a star. There followed a long line of spectaculars which carried the actress's name around the world.

Her screen credits include: *Romeo And Juliet*, Fox, 1916; *Cleopatra*, Fox, 1917; *Madame Du Barry*, Fox, 1917; *Salome*, Fox, 1918; *The She Devil*, Fox, 1918; *The Light*, Fox, 1918; *La Belle Russe*, Fox, 1919.

William Fox spared no expense in these great costume spectaculars and Theda Bara became one of the greatest drawing cards and sex symbols of the silent era. It can be truthfully said that she personified all that was "daring sex" from 1916 into the Twenties.

Romeo And Juliet, (Fox, 1916). Harry Hilliard a New York stage actor played Romeo to Theda Bara's Juliet. The Shakespearean classic was portrayed with full emphasis placed upon the emotional and sexy.

Cleopatra, (Fox, 1917).
In this action scene from the picture Theda Bara and Paul Panzer seemed to be highly perturbed from the stern edict of Anthony. This particular version of the story is probably the very first one on the screen preceding DeMille's version, with Claudette Colbert, Vivian Leigh's English version and the last last one with Elizabeth Taylor and Richard Burton.

Madame DuBarry, (Fox, 1917).
In this famous old classic of French royalty Theda Bara played the title role. Again, this version was probably one of the very first to be done in pictures. The William Fox Studios were at the height of their production standards and were turning these pictures out at a great rate in comparison to modern techniques.

The She Devil, (Fox, 1918).
This particular picture followed along her usual siren pattern.

Salome, (Fox, 1918).
In this action scene from the picture Theda Bara is shown in one of her most seductive poses as she does her dance before John the Baptist's head.

LIONEL BARRYMORE

Born: April 28, 1878, Philadelphia, Penn. Died: 1954. Height: 6'. Weight: 155 lbs. Dark hair and blue eyes. Lionel was the son of Maurice Barrymore, long famous on the stage, and Georgia Drew Barrymore, brilliant comedienne. He made his stage debut as a baby appearing with his parents. He was educated in New York, then joined a touring stock company. He gave up the stage to study painting in Paris for three years. On the New York stage he scored tremendous hits in *The Copperhead, The Jest, Peter Ibbetson, Macbeth, The Claw* and many other plays.

His first screen work was done in early Biograph films. In 1909 D. W. Griffith induced him to play a role in *Friends* and from that time on he gravitated between the screen and the stage. When talking pictures came in he was under contract to M.G.M. and his first talking role in *The Lion And The Mouse* created a sensation. *Alias Jimmy Valentine* and other successes followed.

Watching the new art develop, Lionel saw where his combined knowledge of stage and screen could be useful in directing and his work as a director in *Madame X* with Ruth Chatterton was a great triumph for him. He also directed *The Rogue Song, Ten Cents A Dance,* and other pictures. Lionel Barrymore had decided to give up acting when plans were made to star Norma Shearer in *A Free Soul.* The tremendously dramatic role of the father appealed to him so strongly that he consented to play it. His work in this role won him the award of the Academy of Arts and Sciences for the best screen performance of the year 1931.

His screen credits include *The Yellow Ticket, Broken Lullaby, Mata Hari, Arsene Lupin, Washington Masquerade, Grand Hotel, Rasputin and The Empress, Looking Forward, Dinner At Eight, Night Flight, Strangers Return* and many others.

LIONEL BARRYMORE

A Free Soul, (M.G.M., 1931). Directed by Clarence Brown Lionel Barrymore walked off with most of the honors in this picture and received an academy award for his fine performance. Norma Shearer's work was also outstanding. Lionel Barrymore's many talents included those of a pianist, composer and etcher.

Grand Hotel, (M.G.M., 1932). This film was one of M.G.M.'s greatest. The cast included practically all of the personalities under contract to the studio. In this scene we see Lionel Barrymore, Lewis Stone, and John Barrymore as they enact their starring roles.

Young Doctor Kildare, (M.G.M., 1938). This film was one of what turned out to be a great series costarring Lionel Barrymore and Lew Ayres.

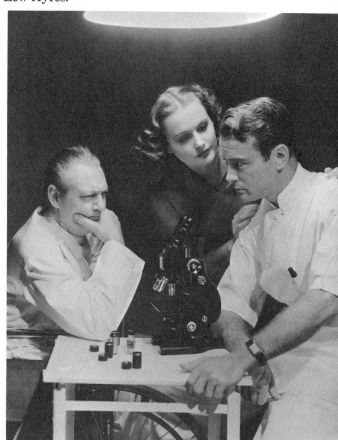

Treasure Island, (M.G.M., 1934). Jackie Cooper played the part of the cabin boy and Lionel Barrymore enacted the role of "Long John Silver." This picture was a great box office success and furthered the careers of both Cooper and Barrymore.

Three Wise Fools, (M.G.M., 1946). Lionel Barrymore costarred with Margaret O'Brian, Grant Mitchell, Edward Arnold and Lewis Stone. This story was one of the modern tear jerkers and these four great veterans of the stage and screen made the most of it.

RICHARD BARTHELMESS

RICHARD BARTHELMESS

Born: New York City, May 9, 1897. Height: 5'9". Weight: 150 lbs. Brown hair and brown eyes. Education: Private and military schools, Trinity College, Hartford, Conn.

His masterpiece was a film called *Tol'Able David*, United Artists. In addition he worked in *The Enchanted Cottage*, *The Amateur Gentleman*, *Classmates*, *The Patent Leather Kid* and *Massacre*. All of these films were under the First National banner. He finished his contract with First National in 1934.

He dates back to the original D. W. Griffith era and his greatest picture with Griffith was *Broken Blossoms* (1919), in which he costarred with Lillian Gish and Donald Crisp.

Tol'Able David, (United Artists, 1921).
One of the greatest films of any and all eras co-starred Richard Barthelmess and Ernest Torrence. This scene depicts one of the greatest fights of all time with Ernest Torrence lying prone in the door-way and Richard Barthelmess, the victor, still in possession of the mail bag.

The Patent Leather Kid, (First National Production, 1927).
In this saga of the first world war, a giant tank almost crushes the "Kid" in a thrilling scene. The story tells of a prize fighter who went on to become a great fighter in the trenches.

The Lash,
(First National and Vitaphone Picture, 1931).
In this story of the early California Dons, Richard Barthelmess costarring with Mary Astor gave one of the first performances of his film career. He also made *The Last Flight* an aviation picture for First National and in 1932 *Cabin In The Cotton.*

Massacre, (First National and Vitaphone Picture, 1934).
Barthelmess portrays an American Indian who, inspite of an American education, is angered by an Indian Government Agent and goes back to the blanket and the breech clout to avenge these injustices to his people. Richard Barthelmess was a student of D. W. Griffith's acting group and under the supervision of Griffith he had previously starred in *The Girl Who Stayed Home, The Idol Dancer* and *Way Down East.*

WARNER BAXTER

Born: March 29, 1893 in Columbus, Ohio. Height: 5'11". Weight: 157 lbs. Brown eyes and dark brown hair.

He came of Ohio pioneer stock which originated in Virginia. At the time Warner was born, his mother was 18 and his father 21. His father died when the child was 5 months old. In 1905, after many moves Warner Baxter attended Polytechnic High School in San Francisco, also the alma mater of Janet Gaynor and George O'Brien.

They were living on a San Francisco hilltop when the 1906 earthquake and fire raized their home. After the fire they re-established their home in San Francisco where Warner secured his first job with the Underwood Typewriter Company.

After many adventures and much traveling out of sheer necessity, he secured a job in a Tulsa stock company, playing juvenile leads at $25 a week and then leading man roles for $35 a week. After a full season of this, in 1914, he headed toward Hollywood and the embryonic movie industry.

He starved trying to crash the movies until Oliver Morosco, who ran a Los Angeles stock company, signed him to a long term contract. When Morosco produced *Lombardi, Ltd.* in New York he took Warner there to play in it. For two years thereafter he toured the country in this play, and returned to live in Hollywood in 1920.

His success in this play got him into pictures. His first important hit was in Fox's first all-talking outdoor production, *In Old Arizona*, for which he won the award of the Academy of Arts and Sciences for his delineation of the Cisco Kid.

He was borrowed by Warners for the lead in *42nd Street*, by M.G.M. for *Penthouse* and Columbia Studios for *Broadway Bill*.

If I Were Queen, (F.B.O. Productions, 1922).
This film was among the very first of the Warner
Baxter group. In it he was the leading man. Ethel
Clayton played the title role as the Queen. Prior to
the time of this film he had spent several years under
contract to Oliver Morosco acting upon the New
York stage and working in Morosco's stock companies throughout the United States. His polished
manners and full projection of his personality were
to immediately make him famous.

Ramona. In this immortal classic of old California,
Baxter was costarred with Dolores Del Rio. The year
was 1928, United Artists Studio produced it and it
rates high amongst Warner Baxter's many fine portrayals.

In Old Arizona, (Fox, 1929).
Warner Baxter was to immortalize himself forever in
his role of the *Cisco Kid* in this film. In this scene
Dorothy Burgess costars with him. 1929 was the sec-
ond year of the Academy Awards, and the Best Actor
Award went to Warner Baxter for this role.

The Prisoner Of Shark Island,
(20th Century-Fox Studios, 1936).

Warner Baxter portrayed a prisoner in a Civil War Union prison. The sadistic sergeant played by John Carradine concocted various methods of torture and punishment to make life unbearable for Baxter. The picture depicts his sufferings, his courage and his various attempts at escape.

The Return of the Cisco Kid,
(20th Century-Fox Picture, 1939).

Baxter returned to the screen with a distinguished cast of Henry Hull, Kane Richmond, C. Henry Gordon and Robert Barrat. In this scene Baxter is costarred with Lynn Bari and Cesar Romero. His fans were legion and demanded over and over again that the *Cisco Kid* "return."

ETHEL MAE BARRYMORE

Born: August 15, 1879, Philadelphia, Penn. Died: Beverly Hills, June 18, 1959.
Ethel Barrymore made her debut in the Empire Theater in New York City in
1884. One of her greatest stage hits was Clyde Fitch's romantic comedy,
Captain Jinks Of The Horse Marines. From then there was never any doubt
that a Barrymore had come into her own. Eventually she was titled "The First
Lady of the American Theater." Her life, her efforts and her conversations were
in, on, and about the theater. She worked in several pictures in 1916 and 1917
but eventually returned to the New York stage.

After many years of great stage success she was persuaded by M.G.M. to
join her brothers, John and Lionel, in *Rasputin and the Empress,* with Ethel
playing the Czarina. In 1944 she returned to Hollywood in *None But The
Lonely Heart* which brought her an Academy Award. From then on she had
a successful screen career. She survived both John and Lionel and was the last
of the fabulous Barrymores.

Her screen credits include twelve miscellaneous silent films from 1914 to
1919 and, of course, with her great stage experience her transition to the
"talkies" was a forgone success. She also did *None But The Lonely Heart,*
R.K.O., 1944; *The Spiral Staircase,* R.K.O., 1946; *Moss Rose,* 20th Century-
Fox, 1947; *The Paradine Case,* Selznick, 1948; *The Great Sinner,* M.G.M.,
1949; *Pinky,* 20th Century-Fox, 1949; *Kind Lady,* M.G.M., 1951; *Dead Line
U.S.A.,* 20th Century-Fox, 1952; *Just For You,* Paramount, 1952; *The Story
Of Three Loves,* M.G.M., 1953; *Young At Heart,* Warner Bros., 1954; *Johnny
Trouble,* Warner Bros., 1957.

Rasputin and the Empress, (M.G.M., 1932).
Ethel Barrymore had been away from the motion picture screen for thirteen years and in this remarkable picture she returned to work with her two brothers, John and Lionel. Her part was that of the Czarina. Lionel played Rasputin and John played the Prince. This was the only picture that the three Barrymores were to perform together. A superb cast included Diana Wynyard, Ralph Morgan, Tad Alexander, C. Henry Gordon, and Edward Arnold.

Night Song, (R.K.O. Radio Picture, 1947). She costarred with Dana Andrews, Merle Oberon, Hoagy Carmichael, Arthur Rubinstein and Eugene Ormandy.

The Great Sinner, (M.G.M., 1949). This screen-play was taken from Dostoevski's *The Gambler* and is considered to be one of her greatest characterizations. In this picture she costarred with Gregory Peck, Ava Gardner, Melvyn Douglas, Walter Huston, Frank Morgan and Agnes Moorehead. In this tense scene we see Ethel Barrymore stake her fortune and her life on a turn of the wheel.

Kind Lady, (M.G.M., 1951). Directed by John Sturges. Ethel Barrymore was in fine company with Maurice Evans, Angela Lansbury, Keenan Wynn, Betsy Blair, John Williams, Doris Lloyd and many others. Maurice Evans played a society crook who attempted to cajole and coerce the old woman out of her fortune and her treasures. Needless to say the crook was not successful.

Young at Heart, (Warner Bros., 1954). Directed by Michael Curtiz; Doris Day and Frank Sinatra starred. The supporting cast included Ethel Barrymore, Gig Young, Dorothy Malone, Elizabeth Fraser and Alan Hale. Ethel Barrymore played the part of the gentle aunt. This was to be almost the close of her brilliant career. One more picture, *Johnny Trouble* (Warner Bros., 1957), would finalize an illustrious lifetime of dedicated service to the theater, radio and the motion pictures.

WALLACE BEERY

WALLACE BEERY

Born: April 1, 1889, Kansas City Mo. Height: 6'1". Weight: 189 lbs. Brown hair and hazel eyes. Educated at Kansas City High School and Chase School in Kansas City.

He joined Ringling's Circus when he was 16. In New York Beery sang in Henry Savage's musical shows in the year of 1904. He started his motion picture career with Essanay in Chicago in 1913 then joined the Keystone Comedy Company and worked with Universal. In a fifty year span he had played in countless pictures. A few of the greatest would be: *Beggars of Life.* 1929; *The Big House*, 1930; *The Champ; Hell Divers; Grand Hotel, Flesh; Tug Boat Annie; Min And Bill;* and *Dinner At Eight.* These last named were among his very best at M.G.M. Let us not forget *Ah Wilderness* and *Treasure Island.* In 1934 he played the title role of Pancho Villa, an M.G.M. Production. He will always be remembered as the deathless "Bill" in *Min And Bill,* a film which immortalized both Marie Dressler and Wallace Beery.

In 1913 Wallace Beery joined the Essanay Film Company and became very famous in the days of the silents in a series of comedies called *The Swedy* series. In this photo we see Wally as the Swedish servant maid with Ruth Stonehouse.

The Champ, (M.G.M., 1931).
In this picture Wallace Beery played an old prize fighter and Jackie Cooper played his son. Wally's predicaments as he tried to bring up his son created an unforgettable film.

Min And Bill, (M.G.M., 1930).
Marie Dressler and Wallace Beery shared the title roles. Breaking all box office records of the 1930's they went on to do *Tug Boat Annie* (M.G.M.).

Viva Villa, (M.G.M., 1934).
Wallace Beery in the title role of this film created one of the greatest performances of his career. Leo Carrillo played his lieutenant and Stu Erwin played the American newspaperman caught in the middle of many perilous situations.

Treasure Island, (M.G.M., 1934).
In this famous pirate story Wallace Beery and Jackie Cooper were teamed up again. Wallace Beery's character as "Long John Silver" was his usual masterly portrayal. Starred with him were Lionel Barrymore and Otto Kruger.

WILLIAM BENDIX

WILLIAM BENDIX

Born: New York City, January 14, 1906. His theatrical career began in 1936 when he did a one night stand as a singing waiter and then secured a job with New Jersey Federal Theater Project. After three years with the Project he worked in six Broadway shows, every one a flop. Considerably more outstanding were his Hollywood roles: *Detective Story, The Babe Ruth Story, The Theater Guilds, The Time Of Your Life* and his greatest masterpiece, the NBC series, *Life Of Riley* for television. Hardy, with a quick laugh and a splendid sense of humor, Bendix was a great favorite among his fellow workers.

Screen credits, beginning in 1942 include: *Brooklyn Orchid, The Last Key, Wake Island, China Hostages, Two Years Before The Mast, Sentimental Journey, Life of Riley, Connecticut Yankee In King Arthur's Court*. Recent pictures were *Cover Up, Johny Holiday, The Gambling House, Submarine Command, Crash Out* and *Battle Stations*.

His unexpected death in 1964 shocked the entire nation. To thousands of loyal fans he will always be "Riley."

A Girl In Every Port, (R.K.O. Radio Picture, 1952).

The McGuerins From Brooklyn,
(Hal Roach—United Artists, 1942).
William Bendix was costarred with Max Baer, Arline Judge, Marjorie Woodworth, Grace Bradley and Joe Sawyer. Bendix performed blundering, idiotic attempts to reduce his weight and become a great athelete. Max Baer the famous ex-heavyweight champion of the world played an important part.

The Life of Riley, (Universal, 1948).
William Bendix starred in this picture from which evolved the original Radio and TV series which was to make his fame and fortune. In this scene the entire cast of the original picture were (left to right): William Bendix, Rosemary De Camp, Richard Long, Mag Randall, Lanny Rees and Mark Daniels.

Kill the Umpire, (Columbia, 1958).
William Bendix played the title role of the umpire as only he could play it. Bendix was a baseball fan and could rattle off averages with the fluency of a sports writer. He once was bat boy for the New York Giants, his favorite team.

The Hairy Ape, (United Artists, 1944).
William Bendix was costarred with Susan Hayward, John Loder and Dorothy Comingore in Eugene O'Neill's play. In this scene William Bendix, Roman Bohnen and Tom Fadden portray the stokers of the ship as they come from the engine rooms.

51

MONTE BLUE

Born: January 11, 1890 in Indianapolis, Indiana. Started with D. W. Griffith as script clerk, actor and stunt man in *Intolerance, The Birth of a Nation,* and *Orphans of the Storm.*

He played mountain boy parts in such pictures as *The Ducklings.* The Warner Bros. Studio gave him a chance at feature leads and stardom soon followed. His screen credits include: *The Marriage Circle, Kiss Me Again, So This Is Paris, Brass, Main Street, Hogan's Alley, Across The Pacific, Across The Atlantic, Wolf's Clothing, Tiger Rose.* He also appeared in *Conquest, From Headquarters.* One of his earlier pictures was *The Affair of Anatole* (Paramount, 1921). He later became one of Hollywood's most successful character actors.

His recent pictures were: *Younger Brothers, Dallas, War Path, Rose of Cimarron, Hangman's Knot, Last Posse* and a part in *Lives of a Bengal Lancer.*

MONTE BLUE

The Affairs of Anatole, (Paramount, 1921). During the twenties, Monte Blue was under contract to the Paramount Studios. In this picture we see him costarred with Alice Joyce, who was originally known as "The Vitagraph Girl." Monte Blue received his education at the Soldiers and Sailors Orphan Home in Knightstown, Indiana. He worked his way through high school and Purdue University.

Tiger Rose, (Warner Bros. Production, 1923). Monte Blue costarred with Lupe Velez in the title role. This film was one of the many fine productions he did while working under contract to Warner Bros.

Conquest, (Warner Bros., 1929). In this air exploration story Monte Blue costarred with H. B. Warner. His start in picture work was on the old Griffith lot where he worked as a ditch digger at $1.50 a day.

Lives of a Bengal Lancer, (Paramount Productions Inc., 1934). Directed by Henry Hathaway, starring Gary Cooper. The cast included: Henry Wilcoxon, Richard Cromwell, Sir Guy Standing, Katherine De Mille, C. Aubrey Smith and Colin Tapley with Monte Blue. This was one of the smash hits of the early talkies.

From Headquarters, (Warner Bros., 1929). Monte Blue and Gladys Brockwell costarred.

MARY BOLAND

Born: January 28, 1880, Detroit, Michigan. Died: June 2, 1965. Height: 5'4". Weight: 125 lbs. Stage credits: *Meet The Wife, Cradle Snatcher, Women Go On Forever, The Vinegar Tree, Face The Music*, and many others. Her screen credits: *Secrets Of A Secretary, Personal Maid, The Night Of June Thirteenth, Trouble In Paradise* and *Evenings For Sale*. All these pictures were made while she was under contract to Paramount Studios.

She did *If I Had A Million, Mama Loves Papa, Three Cornered Moon, Solitaire Man* (M.G.M.), *Ruggles Of Red Gap, Pride And Prejudice* and *Julia Misbehaves*. In the year of 1954 she went back to the New York stage and played in *Lullaby*.

Mary Boland was a great comedienne who developed into a smoothly polished character woman. Her parts were always light, vivacious and gay. She will always be remembered for her immortal work in *Ruggles Of Red Gap* with Charles Ruggles.

MARY BOLAND

If I Had A Million,
(Paramount, 1932).
This picture starred Gary Cooper and George Raft but in various segments the entire Paramount roster was used. Charles Ruggles and Mary Boland played the recipients of the mythical "million."

Six Of A Kind, (Paramount Pictures, Directed by Leo McCarey, 1933).
Besides the usual team of Charles Ruggles and Mary Boland, the great W. C. Fields, Alison Skipworth and George Burns and Gracie Allen were included.

People Will Talk, (Paramount Pictures, 1935).
This picture in which she costarred with Charles Ruggles was the start of a series of films working with Ruggles. She worked in ten or more pictures with him and this superb comedy team turned out to be a smashing success. Included in the cast were: Leila Hyams and Dean Jagger. This picture was directed by Alfred Santell.

Early To Bed, (Paramount Studios, 1936).
Again the famous team of Ruggles and Boland worked together in their tenth picture as a team for Paramount Productions.

Ruggles Of Red Gap, (Paramount Pictures, 1935).
Mary Boland was teamed with Charles Ruggles in one of the greatest comedy casts ever assembled: Charles Laughton, Leila Hyams, Zasu Pitts and Roland Young. This picture was to break all box office records.

HUMPHREY BOGART

HUMPHREY BOGART

Born: New York City, December 25, 1900. Died: January 14, 1957. Educated at Andover Academy. Served in the U.S. Navy World War I.

His stage play credits include: *Swifty, Meet The Wife, Cradle Snatcher, Saturday's Children, Most Immoral Lady* and *Petrified Forest.*

His picture credits include: *Up The River, Body And Soul, Bad Sister, Holy Terror, Love Affair, Petrified Forest, Devil With Women, Dead Reckoning, Big Sleep, Dark Passage, Treasure of Sierra Madre, Key Largo, Knock On Any Door, Tokyo Joe, Chain Lightning, The Enforcer, Sirocco, The African Queen.*

His last pictures were: *Beat The Devil, Caine Mutiny, Sabrina, Barefoot Contessa, We're No Angels, Left Hand Of God, Desperate Hours* and *The Harder They Fall.*

He immortalized himself permanently in *Petrified Forest* where he played "Duke" the desperate gangster and as "Duke" he will always be remembered by the enormous following which avidly watched every film that he made until his death in 1957.

The Petrified Forest, (Warner Bros., 1936).

Humphrey Bogart in his stage career had worked in the stage version of *ThePetrified Forest.* As a result he gave one of the finest performances of his career as "Duke." His fellow artists in this picture were: Charles Grapewin, Genevive Tobin, Paul Harvey, Leslie Howard and Bette Davis. In this tense scene from *Petrified Forest* we see practically the whole cast.

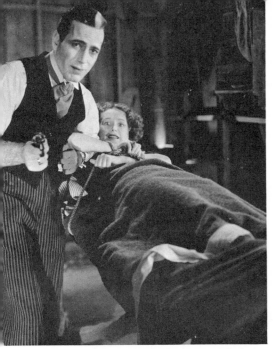

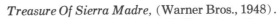
Treasure Of Sierra Madre, (Warner Bros., 1948).
In this story of a search for Mexican gold, Humphrey Bogart was hard pressed to dominate the film. Walter Huston, that famous veteran of stage and screen, played the part of a grizzled old prospector and Tim Holt played Bogart's partner. The film proved to be one of his greatest smash hits.

The Return Of Doctor X,
(Warner Bros. First National, 1939).
Humphrey Bogart was teamed with Wayne Morris and Rosemary Lane. In this action photo we see him in one of his gangster characters.

Key Largo,
(Warner Bros. First National Picture, 1948).
This picture had a very distinguished cast: Edward G. Robinson, Lauren Bacall and Humphrey Bogart with many other contract players on the Warner Bros. lot.

The African Queen, (United Artists, 1951).
Bogart starred with an old boat and Katharine Hepburn playing the part of an old maid. For this work in the film, Bogart won the coveted Academy Award as the Best Actor in the year of 1951.

BOB BURNS

BOB BURNS

Born: August 2, 1896, Van Buren, Arkansas. When Bob made his first bazooka out of two pieces of gas pipe and a whiskey funnel, little did he realize that the basso blasts of the bazooka would be heard around the world. Bob told many tall tales of hill billy folks who could kick boulders for footballs, without bruising their toes; who could stand on hot coals barefoot without knowing there was any fire near; folks who could be lulled to sleep by a chorus of mighty mosquitoes drilling right down into the marrow of their bones.

In vaudeville he was known as "The Arkansas Philosopher." He became very successful in radio and naturally gravitated into the motion pictures. His humorous style of narration and his homespun, Arkansas, hill billy diction turned out to be just as devastating in Hollywood as in vaudeville.

He was one of the very few actors who realized the potentials of the San Fernando Valley real estate. He put all his personal fortune into it and bought up large parcels of acreage. In the course of a very few years he became independently wealthy and retired.

The Big Broadcast Of 1937, (Paramount Productions).
Directed by Mitchell Leisen. In this scene we see Bob Burns, Gracie Allen and George Burns. This great musical included: Martha Raye, Benny Goodman and Leopold Stokowski with their orchestras, Shirley Ross, Ray Milland with Elinor Whitney.

The Arkansas Traveler, (Paramount Productions, Inc., 1938).
Bob Burns played the title role, ably assisted by Fay Bainter, John Beal, Irvin S. Cobb, Jean Parker, Lyle Talbot, Dickie Moore and Porter Hall.

Waikiki Wedding,
(Paramount Pictures, Inc., 1937).
Bing Crosby starred in this picture with Bob Burns, Martha Raye, Shirley Ross, George Barbier and Leif Erikson. Frank Tuttle directed this film. Bob Burns and Martha Raye were discovered to be a great comedy team and worked together in more Paramount Pictures.

Our Leading Citizen,
(Paramount Pictures, 1939).
Bob Burns played the starring role in this picture too with a very fine cast including: Susan Hayward, Joseph Allen, Charles Bickford, Gene Lockhart and Elizabeth Patterson. This picture was directed by Al Santell.

The Hill Billy Deacon, (1942).
Bob Burns played the part of the hill billy deacon and the supporting cast included Jack Carson, Dennis O'Keefe, Mischa Auer, Peggy Moran, Guinn Williams with Ed Brophy. In this scene we see the Hill Billy Deacon showing Ed Brophy that he has lost his money in a little card game.

EDDIE CANTOR

Born: January 31, 1893 in New York City. Height: 5′ 8″. Weight: 142 lbs. Black hair, black eyes. Educated in public schools. At the age of fourteen he made his debut at the Clinton Music Hall. Later he joined Gus Edwards "Kid Cabaret," an act including Lila Lee, Eddy Buzzell and George Jessell, Georgie Price, and Walter Winchell.

His first great step to success was in Ziegfield's "Midnight Frolic." From this famous roof show Eddie was promoted to a featured role in the Annual Ziegfield Follies. Cantor was a fixture in the famous Follies for several seasons, appearing with Will Rogers, W. C. Fields and other favorites. His last appearances in the Follies was his greatest stage success in *Whoopee*, 1928.

At the time Eddie opened in *Whoopee* he was reputed to be one of the richest men in show business. Then came the stock market crash of 1929 which completely wiped out his fortune. Starting from scratch to recoup his losses Cantor turned to the movies. In 1930 he signed with Samuel Goldwyn to appear in a film version of *Whoopee*; the huge success of the picture brought about a deal with Goldwyn whereby Cantor was to make one picture a year. Since then he has made such hits as *Kid Boots, Special Delivery, Palmy Days, The Kid From Spain, Roman Scandals, Kid Millions, Strike Me Pink, Ali Baba Goes To Town, Thank Your Lucky Stars,* and *Hollywood Canteen*. For R.K.O. he not only starred in, but also produced both *Show Business* and *If You Knew Susie*.

EDDIE CANTOR

Palmy Days,
(Samuel Goldwyn Studios, United Artists, 1931).

Eddie Cantor teamed up with Charlotte Greenwood and the famous Goldwyn beauties to produce this great musical. The little guy with the big eyes and the big heart was born on the east side of New York. His father was a violinist. Eddie didn't remember him, for both his mother and father died before Eddie was two years old. He was raised by his grandmother, Esther, who died in 1917, only a few hours before his debut in the Ziegfield Follies.

60

Roman Scandals,
(Sam Goldwyn Production,
United Artists, 1933).
Edward Arnold and Eddie Cantor carried this film to the heights of absurdity. This picture is considered one of Cantor's greatest musicals and gained him thousands of followers.

Thank Your Lucky Stars,
(Warner Bros. First National Picture, 1943).
In this scene Eddie Cantor and Cuddles Sakall carry on in front of the chorus line. Years later Warner Bros. was to produce the saga of his life, aptly titled, *The Eddie Cantor Story.* Though the role of *Eddie* was enacted by Keefe Brasselle, Eddie actually did all the singing.

Kid Millions,
(Samuel Goldwyn Production,
United Artists, 1934).
Kid Millions was destined to be one of Cantor's greatest musicals.

Samuel Goldwyn was noted and respected by the film industry for a very high quality of motion picture production. All of his films bore this unmistakable stamp of quality and cleanliness. Goldwyn's greatest masterpiece is considered to be *The Best Years Of Our Lives* starring Fredric Marsh and Myrna Loy in a moving story of a soldier back from the war.

Show Business,
(An R.K.O. Radio Picture, 1950).
This picture was to team Joan Davis and Eddie Cantor with George Murphy playing the straight man. Following *Show Business* he also produced and acted in *If You Knew Susie,* 1948. These two were his only pictures with R.K.O. During this time this energetic comedian found time to write an autobiographical book, *My Life Is In Your Hands,* and short humorous works such as *Caught Short,* (making fun of his life's savings in the 1929 stock market crash) and *Yoo, Hoo Prosperity,* (about the depression).

RUTH CHATTERTON

RUTH CHATTERTON

Born: December 24, 1893 in New York City. Height: 5'2½". Weight: 110 lbs. Light brown hair and blue eyes. She was educated at Pellam Manor, leaving there when she was fourteen years old to play a part in a stage production. She sought and obtained a place with a stock company playing in Washington, D. C., while she was spending her school holidays in that city. Her first part was that of a cockney chorus girl. After this successful start she gained a place in stock with Lowell Sherman, playing with Pauline Lord and Lenore Ulric.

Her rise was exceptionally rapid, and when she was eighteen years old, she was being starred. Her last outstanding role before stardom came as leading woman for Henry Miller in *Daddy Long Legs*; following that she was starred in *Moon Light and Honey Suckle* and then was costarred with Henry Miller. While she was playing in *The Devil's Plum Tree* in a Los Angeles theater, Emil Jannings, the great German Actor, saw her work. Her first screen role was in Jannings' Paramount Picture *Sins Of The Fathers*.

Her Paramount Screen credits are: *Sins Of The Fathers; The Doctor's Secret; The Dummy; Charming Sinners; The Laughing Lady; Sarah And Son;* and *Paramount On Parade; Madame X,* (M.G.M.); *Anybody's Woman; Once A Lady; Frisco Jenny; Lilly Turner;* and *Dodsworth,* a Samuel Goldwyn Production.

This picture, *Dodsworth,* is considered to be her greatest performance on the screen.

Sarah And Son,
(Paramount Picture, 1930).
Ruth Chatterton and Fredric March starred in this famous story of mother love with Miss Chatterton carrying off all the acting honors.

Once A Lady, (Paramount Pictures, 1931).
In this film she was supported by Ivor Novello, Jill Esmond and Geoffrey Kerr. This film was to be one of many in which she played a girl of uncertain morals and shady backgrounds.

The Magnificent Lie, (Paramount, 1931).
Charles Boyer was in the greatest demand as one of the finest leading men of his time. He costarred with Ruth Chatterton in this film. Combining the two stars great drawing power, this picture proved a great success at the box office.

Lilly Turner,
(Warner Bros. Studios First National Production, 1933).
In this era George Brent was under contract to Warner Bros. and was one of the most successful leading men of the Thirties. He costarred with Ruth Chatterton and they proved to be a very successful team.

Dodsworth, (Samuel Goldwyn Productions United Artists, 1936).
From Sinclair Lewis' great book *Dodsworth*, Samuel Goldwyn filmed the story with a terrific cast consisting of: Ruth Chatterton, Walter Huston, David Niven, Mary Astor, Paul Lukas and John Payne.

JACK CARSON

JACK CARSON

Born: Carmen, Canada, October 27, 1910. Height: 6′1″. Weight: 220 lbs. Blue eyes and brown hair.

He was educated at the Hartford School in Milwaukee, at St. John's Military Academy at Delafield, Wisconsin, and Carleton College. He got into a theatrical career at the age of nineteen when a fellow student at Carleton College in Northfield, Minn. said "Say, we'll make a funny team; let's go on the stage." They went from small time to Broadway before splitting the act and going their separate ways.

Vaudeville died, and Carson came to Hollywood. After some bit parts he was placed under contract to Warner Bros. and appeared in many of their comedies and soon was a full fledged star.

His screen credits are: *A Legal Bride; Mister Universe; Bright Leaf; The Good Humor Man; My Dream Is Yours; It's A Great Feeling; Two Guys From Milwaukee; Mildred Pierce; The Dough Girls; Hollywood Canteen Make Your Own Bed; One More Tomorrow; Shine On Harvest Moon; Thank Your Lucky Stars*, etc.

Shine On Harvest Moon,
(A Warner Bros. First National Picture, 1944).

This title was from the famous song by Jack Norworth and was made into a comedy with Jack Carson and Marie Wilson costarring.

April Showers,
(A Warner Bros. First National, 1948).
In this picture Ann Sothern and Jack Carson
played leads. Jack Carson could play almost any
musical instrument by ear but preferred the piano.
At home he enjoyed himself laying bricks and gar-
dening. He liked bridge, poker and arguments. He
was not interested in clothes. His suppressed desire
was to rid people of inhibitions. Most of his discus-
sions involved psychology.

It's A Great Feeling,
(A Warner Bros. Technicolor Production, 1949).
Jack Carson was costarred with Dennis Morgan
and Doris Day. As a hobby Jack Carson collected
wooden figures and put them on mantelpieces all
over the house. He had a definite financial program
and a business manager, who attended to all of
Carson's financial affairs. Jack owned a 48 acre
ranch in Woodland Hills, well-stocked with a wide
assortment of animals and poultry.

Two Guys From Milwaukee,
(A Warner Bros. First National Film, 1946).
Jack Carson and Dennis Morgan costarred with Janis Paige,
Pattie Brady and Joan Leslie. His appearances in many Warner
Bros. comedies won him better and better roles as the months
rolled by, and the many different types of roles only served to
prove his versatility.

John Loves Mary, (A Warner Bros. Picture, 1948).
In this film Ronald Reagan and Patricia Neal costarred and Jack
Carson supplied the comedy relief. Jack Carson's favorite foods
were "most of those I shouldn't eat." He had to watch his weight,
but had no trouble reducing. He played golf, with a nine handi-
cap, swam for outdoor recreation and liked to attend prize fights.

LON CHANEY

Born: April 1, 1883, Colorado Springs, Colorado. Died: 1930. Height: 5'9". Weight: 155 lbs. Black hair and brown eyes.

Stage experience was gained as the producer of *The Little Tycoon* with his brother in 1899. He worked on the stage as actor, property man and transportation agent. His era in motion pictures was a remarkable one because he worked before the days of a make-up man. In the very early part of his movie career he quickly learned that his talent and forte were in the macabre, the ghastly, weird, grotesque and misshapen; as a result his nickname was "the master of make-up."

His screen credits include: *The Miracle Man*, 1919; *Outside The Law*, 1921; *The Trap*, 1922; *The Hunchback Of Notre Dame* and *The Shock*, 1923; *Phantom Of The Opera*, Universal 1925; *Treasure Island*, Paramount, 1921; *The Penalty*, Goldwyn, 1921. Under contract with M.G.M. he made *He Who Gets Slapped*, *Tower Of Lies*, *The Monster*, *The Unholy Three* in 1925; *The Black Bird*, *The Road To Mandalay*, *Tell It To The Marines* in 1926; *Mr. Wu*, *The Unknown*, *Mockery* in 1927; *Laugh Clown Laugh*, *While The City Sleeps*, *West Of Zanzibar* in 1928; *Thunder*, *Where East Is East* in 1929 and *The Unholy Terror*, 1930.

In order not to hold up a picture, he worked when he was ill. He never spared himself and readily endured agonies to perfect one of his distorted and macabre characterizations. He constantly invented devices to cripple his strong body for his roles, and tried dangerous experiments in order to obtain the weird effects he demanded in his desire for perfection.

LON CHANEY

The Miracle Man, (Paramount Art Craft, 1919). Lon Chaney costarred with Betty Compson and Thomas Meighan. This picture was one of the greatest box office smash hits of its time and created immediate stardom for Chaney, Compson and Meighan.

Hunchback Of Notre Dame, (Universal, 1923).
Lon Chaney horrified the entire nation as he played the part of Quasimodo the misshapen dwarf. Patsy Ruth Miller was costarred with him.

Phantom Of The Opera, (Universal, 1925).
Lon Chaney played the title role and scaled new heights in horror make-up when his scenes showed the burnt and scarred face of Erick the Phantom. The dramatic scene in which Mary Philbin tears the mask from his face and the sudden close-up caused women to faint in the theaters all over the land. Norman Kerry played Mary Philbin's lover.

The Unholy Three, (M.G.M., 1930).
This story was about an unholy alliance between three different kind of crooks. The midget Perry Arles and Ivan Linow completed the trio. This was Chaney's last picture. He died in this same year, 1930.

London After Midnight,
(Metro Goldwyn Mayer, 1927).
Lon Chaney played the part of the mad hypnotist and his horrible make-up, included an innovation of filed teeth.

JEFF CHANDLER

Born: December 5, 1918, Brooklyn, New York. Height: 6'4". Weight: 210 lbs. Brown eyes and iron grey hair.

While he was still a boy his family moved across the East River to Manhattan and he was graduated from high school there. While in high school Jeff resolved to become an actor but he couldn't do much to satisfy his desire. His mother ran a small candy and stationery store and Jeff had to help out after school hours. Consequently he had no time to participate in any of the school dramatic activities. He received a scholarship with the Feagin School of Dramatic Art in New York, which was granted him in return for doing a certain amount of work around the school. After completing his dramatic course he went to work with a Long Island Stock Company. He spent four years in the Army in the last World War. After receiving his discharge December 6, 1945, he decided to come to Hollywood to try his luck in the movies.

He became very successful in the radio field and through the radio medium he received his long awaited break in pictures. His first picture was *The Sword In The Desert* and before the film was half finished he was placed under a long term contract.

His screen credits include: *Abandoned; Deported; Two Flags West; Broken Arrow; Smuggler's Island; Bird Of Paradise; Iron Man; Flame Of Araby; The Battle At Apache Pass; Red Ball Express; Yankee Buccaneer; Because Of You; The Great Sioux Uprising; East Of Sumatra; War Arrow; Yankee Pasha; Sign Of The Pagan; Foxfire; Female On The Beach; The Spoilers; Away All Boats; Pillars Of The Sky; Toy Tiger; Durango; The Tattered Dress; Pay The Devil; The Lady Takes A Flyer;* and *Raw Wind In Eden.*

JEFF CHANDLER

His sudden and untimely death on June 17, 1961 shocked his great following and the motion picture world. He was at the top of the heap, one of the greatest actors of his era with unlimited potentials of a fine career ahead of him when he passed on.

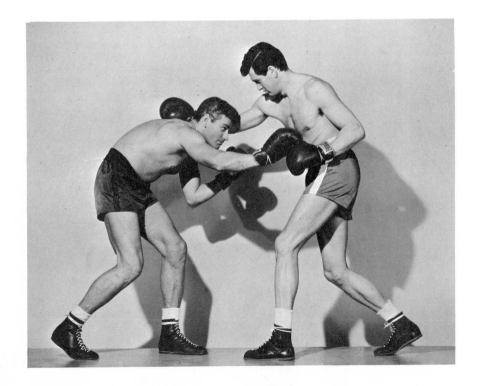

Iron Man,
(Universal Studios, 1951).
In this picture Jeff Chandler and Rock Hudson were co-starred with Evelyn Keyes and Stephen McNally. In this tale of the prize fights the tremendous physique of Jeff Chandler showed to good advantage and spurred him on his way to stardom.

Red Ball Express, (Universal Pictures Company, 1952).
This Army story was old stuff to Jeff Chandler in the light
of his four years of actual Army service.

Jeanne Eagles, (Columbia Pictures, 1957).
This tragic story and great biographical film depicted
the life, career and loves of one of our greatest
American actresses. Kim Novak and Jeff Chandler
ran the romantic gamut of tender love, bitter argument
and sharp separation in the George Sidney production.

Thunder In The Sun, (Paramount Studios, 1959).
In this Western story of the early pioneers, Susan Hayward, Jacques Bergerac costarred with Jeff Chandler
to create a stirring, vivid picture of violence, action,
tragedy and love.

The Spoilers, (Universal, International, 1955).
Anne Baxter and Rory Calhoun starred with Jeff Chandler
in Rex Beach's adventure classic. A "must" in the many versions of "The Spoilers" was of course the great fight scene —
in this version — between Chandler and Calhoun. The violence and action of this fight is considered to be on a par with
the original fight between William Farnum and Tom Santchi.

SYDNEY CHAPLIN

No One To Guide Him,
(Mack Senett—Keystone Comedy, 1915).
Sydney Chaplin also belonged to that great, illustrious group of Mack Sennett Players, and we see him in this scene playing the part of a bartender-waiter serving Edgar Kennedy. In later comedies he was to work with his brother, Charlie.

The Better 'Ole, (World Productions, 1919).
Sydney Chaplin played the part of the typical English soldier in *The Better 'Ole.* It was the best part of his entire career and was his finest hour of acting. Only an Englishman who had actually lived through these experiences could have done full justice to this part. After doing this picture, Sydney Chaplin was to return to the comedy routines of the Mack Sennett players but never again was he to reach the heights of inspired genius and turn out another picture such as this one.

SYDNEY CHAPLIN

Born: Capetown, South Africa. Died: 1965. Height: 5'7½". Weight: 150 lbs. Dark hair and brown eyes. His boyhood and education were in London, England. He acquired his stage training in London in Music Halls. Upon learning of his brother, Charles Chaplin's phenomenal success in the film comedy field, he came to America and also became a famous film comedian.

His film credits include: *Man On The Box; Charley's Aunt; The Better 'Ole;MissingLink; Fortune Hunter; Skirts; Oh, What A Nurse* and many others. After a very successful career, he retired and returned to London, England to reside there permanently. According to legend, it was Sydney Chaplin's business acumen which was instrumental in guiding Charlie Chaplin's footsteps to financial security and making sure that Charles Chaplin received the full monetary benefits from his great successes. Sydney Chaplin's interpretation of the typical English Tommy in his World War I comedy is considered to be his finest and greatest role.

Charley's Aunt, (Producers Distributing Corporation, 1925). This was to be the first version of *Charley's Aunt*. Columbia was to do *Charley's Aunt* in 1930, and Jack Benny developed one of his most successful comedies from his interpretation of *Charley's Aunt* for 20th Century Fox in 1941. We must also mention Ray Bolger's version, *Where's Charley?* (Warner Brothers).

Off The Trail (Scene of Syd & Charlie Chaplin together). The Brothers Chaplin were to leave their mark upon the Hollywood scene. Fame and fortune in no small degree came their way, and Charlie's phenomenal success under the guiding business hand of Syd were to place them far beyond the privations and poverty of their tragic boyhoods.

The Fortune Hunter, (Warner Brothers, 1928). Sydney Chaplin was placed under contract to Warner Brothers and made a few successful pictures there.

LINDA DARNELL

Born: October 16, 1921, Dallas, Texas. Died: April 10, 1965. She was a Texas-born beauty who had long been described as "The girl with the perfect face." She was a Hollywood star for better than twenty-five years. At the age of fifteen she was the youngest leading lady in Hollywood history. She was a fourteen year old student at Sunset High School, Dallas, Texas when a 20th Century Fox talent scout spotted her and arranged a screen test in Hollywood. Over a year after her first test Hollywood Producer, Darryl Zanuck called for her return to play the leading feminine role in a picture and she immediately rose to the heights of stardom.

Her stage credits included: *Monique; Critics Choice; Gioconda Smile; The Royal Family; Late Love;* and many others. Her TV credits were: *Playhouse 90; Climax; Wagon Train;* and *Cimarron City.* Her screen credits were: *Stardust; Mark Of Zorro; Blood And Sand; City Without Men; It Happened Tomorrow, Unfaithfully Yours; Forever Amber; Letter To Three Wives;* and *Everybody Does It.* Recent pictures: *The Thirteenth Letter; Island Of Desire; Blackbeard The Pirate; This Is My Love,* etc.

We shall always remember her as the vivacious vixen in the early days of merry old England in *Forever Amber.*

LINDA DARNELL

Hangover Square,
(20th Century Fox, 1945).
Linda Darnell was costarred with Laird Cregar and George Sanders with a supporting cast of Glenn Langan, Fay Marlowe and Alan Napier. This film was one of the morbid murder-mystery type and proved big box office with such a distinguished cast.

72

Centennial Summer,
(20th Century Fox, 1946).
In this picture she was costarred with Lillian
Gish. From the time of her movie debut in 1939
until 1964 she had starred in more than fifty
motion pictures.

Forever Amber, (20th Century Fox, 1947).
A Technicolor picture. Cornel Wilde costarred with Linda
Darnell in this film. In this picture she reached the height
of her acting career.

Blackbeard The Pirate, (R.K.O. Radio Picture, 1952).
A Technicolor epic. In this dramatic action scene we see
Irene Ryan, of Beverly Hillbillies TV fame, at the left.
Keith Andes, who played the romantic male lead, William
Bendix who played the part of Blackbeard's first mate
and Blackbeard as portrayed by Robert Newton.

My Darling Clementine,
(20th Century Fox, 1946).
Victor Mature and Henry Fonda costarred
with Linda Darnell in this rollicking comedy.
In her many many years as a top flight motion
picture star she worked with all the leading
men and contempories of her era.

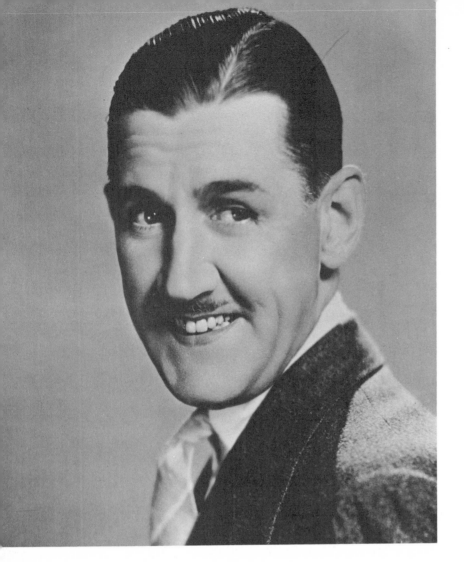

CHARLES CHASE

Born: October 20, 1893. Died: 1940. Birthplace: Baltimore, Maryland. Height: 6'. Weight: 155 lbs. Brown hair and blue eyes. At the age of sixteen in 1909, Charlie Chase was singing the popular songs of the day illustrated with lantern slides in the little movie houses. He learned some dance steps and later went into vaudeville and musical comedy as a song and dance man.

In 1912 Mack Sennett gave Charlie Chase a job as a Keystone Cop. Shortly afterwards Mr. Chase began to direct for the Sennett and other studios and did not appear on the screen again for ten years. In 1925, while directing for Hal Roach, the erstwhile song and dance comedian was persuaded to act once more. As a screen comedian he was so well received by the public that Charlie Chase comedies became one of the big features of Hal Roach's two reel comedy product.

He was one of the very few actors who was also successful as a writer and a director. His screen credits include his very successful series of Hal Roach comedies and in 1929 he worked in *Modern Love*, *You Can't Buy Love*, *Stepping Out* and *Leaping Love*.

All Parts, (Metro Goldwyn Mayer-Hal Roach Comedy).

In this film Charlie Chase costarred with Edgar Kennedy, another great comedian of the Hal Roach alumni, and this team formed an unbeatable combination of funny gags and impossible situations.

Long Live The King,
(Hal Roach Comedies).

Be Your Age.
Charlie Chase costarred with Oliver Hardy who had just been placed under contract to the Hal Roach studios and had not yet formed the immortal partnership of "Laurel and Hardy." Charlie's hobbies were golf and music and he could play many musical instruments, had a very fine voice and was a professional dancer.

In this particular picture, title unknown, we see Charlie Chase having the good fortune to have Thelma Todd as his feminine lead. Her untimely death a few years later left Hollywood with one of its many unsolved mysteries.

The Lighter That Failed,
(A Metro Goldwyn Mayer—Hal Roach Comedy).
It had become the custom of many of the comedy studios to lampoon and satirize the dramatic spectaculars; this particular comedy was a satire on Rudyard Kipling's great story "The Light That Failed."

75

LEW CODY

Born: February 22, 1891, Waterville, Maine. Died: June 1, 1934. Height: 5' 11". Weight: 176 lbs. Black hair and brown eyes. He owned five stock companies, toured vaudeville, performed stock in *The Great Divide, The Last Crown, Within The Law* and others.

His screen credits include: *A Branded Soul*, 1915; *Treasure of The Sea*, Fox 1917; *Don't Change Your Husband*, Art Craft 1919; *The Beloved Christian*, 1920; *The Sign of The Door*, First National 1921; *Reno*, Goldwin 1924; *Revelation*, M.G.M.; *What a Widow*, Pathe; *By Appointment Only*, Paramount.

His most popular role was that of a man about town, the debonair, roistering hero. He lived his own life to the fullest. His career spanned the early days of the Silents and he also successfully made the transition into the talkies. His many starring roles have made him a legendary figure of both the silent and the talking screen.

LEW CODY

The Life Line, (Paramount Art Craft Picture— Maurice Tourneur Production, 1919).
This picture was made while he was under contract to Paramount.

Dishonored, (Paramount, 1931).
Victor McLaglen and Marlene Dietrich costarred with Lew Cody in this box office success. This film was directed by Josef von Sternberg

76

By Appointment Only,
(Cohen Features, 1933).
Aileen Pringle played the feminine lead to Lew Cody's starring role. Cody was noted for his readiness in aiding charitable affairs or initiating plans to make any celebration a success.

Shoot The Works, (Paramount Productions, 1934).
This story of flag pole sitters, honky-tonk girls, out-of-tune orchestras, flea circuses and whale exhibitors, all whirling around Jack Oakie as Nicky the great lover of the midways and byways had Dorothy Dell playing the Lilly of the story. Lew Cody, Ben Bernie, Arline Judge, Alison Skipworth, and Paul Cavanagh costarred.

Lew Cody married Dorothy Dalton who divorced him in 1916. Not until 1926 did his romance with Mabel Normand culminate in marriage at Ventura, California on September 17. They were destined to have only a few years of happiness however, for three years after their marriage she was stricken with tuberculosis. At the same time Cody was desperately ill although knowledge of his illness was kept from her. Mabel died in 1930 and Lew Cody died in 1934.

RONALD COLMAN

RONALD COLMAN

Birthplace: Richmond, Surrey, England. Born: February 9, 1891. Height: 5' 11". Weight: 153 lbs. Brown Hair, brown eyes. He served in the First World War as a member of Kitchener's Army, seeing action in the Great Battle of Ypres, France. He was disabled at Messines. After the war he tried all kinds of jobs, eventually interesting himself in the theater as a career. Restive and dissatisfied with his progress he decided in 1920 to come to America. Landing in New York fortified with fifty-seven dollars in cash, three clean collars and two letters of introduction, he rented a small room in Brooklyn and took the subway to Manhattan in his daily haunting of the agencies and production offices.

Following two years of "Extra" work and small parts Colman finally got his first break in an important supporting role in the Schubert production of *La Dendresse* starring Ruth Chatterton and Henry Miller. He was discovered in this by Henry King, the noted screen director, who gave him the leading male role opposite Lillian Gish in the *White Sister*.

Colman was an instant hit and was immediately starred in *Romolo*. His screen credits include: *A Double Life, The Late George Apley, Kismet, Random Harvest, The Talk Of The Town, The Light That Failed, Prisoner Of Zenda, Under Two Flags, Raffles, Beau Geste, Clive of India, Condemned, Lost Horizon, Tale Of Two Cities, Arrowsmith, Stella Dallas, Kiki*, and others.

His outstanding and unforgettable role in *Arrowsmith* has made him an immortal of the screen, even though he won the Oscar in 1946 as Best Actor.

Arrowsmith, (United Artists, 1931).
This film proved to be one of Colman's greatest. In it he was costarred with Helen Hayes, one of the finest New York actresses of the century. In *Arrowsmith* from Sinclair Lewis' book, Colman plays his usual light-hearted lover until the tragic death of his wife in the film.

Lost Horizon, (Columbia, 1937).
Ronald Colman was supported by a very fine cast: H. B. Warner played the Grand Lama and Jane Wyatt also played a fine part.

The Prisoner Of Zenda, (Selznick International, 1937).
In this film Ronald Colman played a king and Madeline Carroll acted the role of a princess. This team was supported by C. Aubrey Smith, Raymond Massey, David Niven, Douglas Fairbanks Jr. and Mary Astor. John Cromwell directed.

Random Harvest, (M.G.M., 1942).
This film was adapted from James Hilton's memorable love story. Greer Garson and Ronald Colman for the first time appeared together. Mervyn LeRoy gave his inspired direction to this film.

Kismet, (M.G.M., 1944).
In this romance of old Bagdad Ronald Colman played the dashing, devious Haji, Beggar-magician who masqueraded as a Prince. Costarred with him was Marlene Dietrich as the exotic and mysterious Lady Jammilla. Edward Arnold headed the supporting cast of great film artists including James Craig, Joy Ann Page, Hugh Herbert, Colbert Cavanaugh, Henry Davenport, Florence Bates and Robert Warwick.

MARION DAVIES

Born: January 3, 1897, New York City. Height: 5'5''. Weight: 120 lbs. Blonde Hair and blue eyes. Educated in a parochial school in Brooklyn and the convent of The Sacred Heart in Hastings, New York. Her beauty caught the attention of a stage producer who put her into the chorus of *Chu Chin Chow*. Then she posed for *The American Girl* of the noted artist, Howard Chandler Christy and Harrison Fisher. While she was on vacation she was photographed by a newsreel photographer in Florida. A motion picture producer saw this news subject, was impressed by the girl's charm on the screen, and gave her a contract to appear in *Runaway Romany*. Her success was immediate and she was a star from the very start of her career.

Her pictures include: *The Belle Of New York, The Restless Sex, The Dark Star, Little Old New York, When Knighthood Was In Flower, Zander The Great, Yolanda, Beverly Of Graustark, The Cardboard Lover, Show People, Marianne, Not So Dumb, The Floradora Girl, Bachelor Father* (1930). *Polly Of The Circus, Blonde Of The Follies, Hearts Divided, Cain And Mabel,* in 1937 *Ever Since Eve,* (Warner Bros.).

She devoted the latter part of her life to many great philanthropies, donating large sums towards hospitals and orphanages.

MARION DAVIES

Cecilia Of The Pink Roses,
(Graphic Film Corp., 1918).

In the early days of the film industry it was customary to have a melodramatic caption with each photo; this scene was no exception. As in the days of yore, Cecilia still watches like a mother over her wayward brother.

Show People, (M.G.M., 1928).
Marion Davies costarred with Polly Moran and William Haines to produce a rollicking comedy of the highest quality.

Page Miss Glory, (Warner Bros., 1935).
Directed by Mervyn LeRoy. This picture enlisted the services of practically all the contract players on the Warner Bros. lot. Heading this superb cast were Marion Davies, Dick Powell, Pat O'Brien, Mary Astor, Frank McHugh, Patsy Kelly, Lyle Talbot, Barton MacLane, Jack Mulhall and many many others.

When Knighthood Was In Flower,
(Cosmopolitan, 1922).
Marion Davies played the part of Princess Mary Tudor. Forrest Stanley enacted the role of Charles Brandon. This picture is acknowledged to be one of her greatest roles.

Peg Of My Heart, (M.G.M., 1934).
Marion Davies starred in this great old classic and the great majority of her faithful followers sincerely believe that this picture was her greatest.

WALTER CONNOLLY

Born: April 8, 1888. Died: 1940. Birthplace: Cincinnati, Ohio. Height: 5'9". Weight: 190 lbs. Brown hair and brown eyes. He had a great acting history and was a noted character actor from the New York legitimate stage.

His screen credits include: *The Bitter Tea Of General Yen, Washington's Merry-Go-Round, Plain Clothes Man, No More Orchids*. He worked for Columbia. In 1933: *Lady For A Day, Master Of Men, East Of Fifth Avenue, A Man's Castle, Paddy, The Next Best Thing*. In 1934: *Eight Girls In A Boat, It Happened One Night*, and others.

The role in which he achieved cinematic immortality was that of the Father in *It Happened One Night.*

WALTER CONNOLLY

Father Brown, Detective,
(Paramount Pictures, 1934).

Costarred was Gertrude Michael, Paul Lukas and Una O'Connor. Walter Connolly played the title role and the picture was directed by Edward Sedgwick. He was under contract to Columbia at the time of this picture and was loaned to Paramount for this one film.

The Music Goes-Round,
(Columbia Pictures Corp., 1936).
Harry Richman, Rochelle Hudson, Douglass Dumbrille and Walter Connolly made a great starring cast for this theatrical story of life among the actors.

The Good Earth, (Metro-Goldwyn-Mayer, 1937).
In Pearl Buck's great novel of Old China, Paul Muni and Luise Rainer costarred with Charles Grapewin and Walter Connolly in the supporting roles.

First Lady,
(Warner Bros. First National Picture, 1937).
Veree Teasvale played the feminine lead with Walter Connolly playing one of his most effective characterizations. Walter Connolly's hobby was collecting antique theater programs.

Victor Herbert, (Paramount Picture, 1939).
Directed by Andrew Stone. Walter Connolly played the title role and the superb cast included: Allan Jones, Mary Martin, Susanna Foster, Jerome Cowan, Judith Barrett and John Garrick.

GARY COOPER

Born: May 7, 1901, Helena, Montana. Died: May 13, 1961. Height: 6'2". Weight: 160 lbs. Reddish brown hair, blue eyes.

He lived in Helena until he was nine years old. At the age of thirteen he suffered injuries in an automobile accident that compelled him to leave school and to recover his health, he went to his Father's cattle ranch in Montana. It was at this time that he gained the experience which qualified him for later stardom in pictures. In 1924, on Thanksgiving Day, he came to Los Angeles with his sketch book under his arm, determined to become a commercial artist. But this venture was none too successful. After three months of struggling, the lure of motion pictures seized him, and he joined the ranks of the aspiring extras. For more than a year, he played atmosphere, and then came his first chance at a real part. He worked for an independent producer on the poverty row of Hollywood to play a bit in a two reeler. Eileen Sedgewick was his first leading woman. After the release of this short film, Cooper's path became easier.

Cooper was summoned to the Paramount Studio and within thirty minutes was offered a long term contract which he accepted. His screen credits at Paramount included: *Children Of Divorce, Wings, Arizona Bound, Nevada, Beau Sabreur, Legion Of The Condemned, Half A Bride, The First Kiss, The Shopworn Angel, Wolf Song, Betrayal, The Virginian, Seven Days Leave, Only The Brave, The Texan, Paramount On Parade, Farewell To Arms, Lives Of A Bengal Lancer.* In *Sergeant York* he won the Academy Award for the best performance of 1941. Again in *High Noon* he won the Academy Award for the Best Actors' Performance of 1952. *For Whom The Bell Tolls* is considered one of his greatest pictures. Among his last pictures were: *Vera Cruz, Friendly Persuasion* and *Love In The Afternoon.*

GARY COOPER

Three Pals, 1925
It was a quickie Western done on "Poverty Row." In this action photo we see Gary Cooper standing nonchalantly at the extreme left watching the hero, the late Jay Frank Glendon. The girl in the picture is Marilyn Mills. This was Gary Cooper's first screen role.

84

Farewell To Arms,
(Paramount, 1932).
In this picture Gary Cooper co-starred with Helen Hayes and Adolphe Menjou. This was from Ernest Hemingway's famous book, and Frank Borzage produced and directed this production. It is considered to be one of Cooper's greatest performances.

Sergeant York,
(Warner Bros. First National, 1941).
In this true story of Sergeant York, Cooper was starring with Walter Brennan and Joan Leslie. In this action photo we see George Tobias, Cooper and Joe Sawyer in the trenches. His performance in this picture earned him the coveted "Oscar" for the Best Actor Performance of 1941.

For Whom The Bell Tolls,
(Paramount Picture, 1943).
In this tale of the Civil War in Spain, Gary Cooper was co-starred with Ingrid Bergman and was ably supported by a very fine cast including: Akim Tamiroff, Katina Paxinou, Arturo DeCordova, Joseph Calleia and many others. Produced in Technicolor by Sam Wood, this film was a record breaker.

High Noon, (United Artists, 1952).

This story of a small Western town with Gary Cooper playing the sheriff and Grace Kelly playing his bride, became Gary's greatest Western film.   The ensuing events with Gary Cooper's eventual victory over his enemies created one of the greatest Western pictures ever done. This film was directed by Fred Zinnemann and in the supporting cast were: Otto Kruger, William Mitchell and Lon Chaney Jr.

This story of World War I created stars out of several of the performers in this picture. John Gilbert and Renee Adoree costarred and Karl Dane played a big supporting role. His characterization of "Slim" the tobacco-chewing dough boy is acknowledged to be his masterpiece.

KARL DANE

Born: October 12, 1886, Copenhagen, Denmark. Height: 6'3½". Weight: 205 lbs. Karl Dane hurdled into film fame and a long term contract with M.G.M. for his work in the *Big Parade*. From this great picture his career was one big success after another. His screen credits are as follows: *The Big Parade; La Boheme; Bardelys, The Magnificent; The Scarlet Letter; Son Of The Sheik; Monte Carlo; The Red Mill; The Trail Of 98; The Duke Steps Out; Alias Jimmy Valentine; The Gob; Hollywood Review Of Reviews* and *Speedway*. He was then teamed up with George K. Arthur, one of the greatest comedians of that time, and they starred in *Rookies; Baby Mine; All At Sea; Detectives; On To Singapore* and *Brotherly Love*.

His untimely death cut short his career at the pinnacle of his greatness. From the *Big Parade* his faithful fans will remember his characterization of "Slim." In this part he earned screen immortality.

Brotherly Love, (M.G.M., 1928).
This film was among the first comedies that teamed Karl Dane and George K. Arthur. In this photo we see a football game in a prison yard. When the starter shoots his pistol for the beginning of the game the boys think a jail break is on and they all raise their hands and stand still.

Baby Mine, (M.G.M., 1928).

Although the acting profession, the theater, and the stage had been bred in Dane's bones since his earliest childhood, he found it far from easy to break into the films when he came to this country at the close of the First World War

Detectives, (M.G.M., 1928).

This picture was only one of many in the series which Arthur and Dane were to do so successfully for M.G.M. Karl Dane's boyhood filled just about every job there was to fill in connection with the theater. He was everything from call and curtain boy to the baby in his Father's productions. He had been on the stage most of his life and he returned to the stage at the outbreak of the First World War.

All At Sea, (M.G.M., 1929).

The biggest part of this picture was done at Fort McArthur, Calif. and in it Arthur and Dane played a pair of fumbling, blundering sailors. When Karl Dane was fifteen years old he left the stage and studied to become a construction engineer. Though he had been on the stage most of his life he often reverted to engineering as a side line. When he came to America he applied for work as an extra at the Eastern Studios. It seemed to be a hopeless ambition until Vitagraph gave him his first "bit." This small part progressed into an important part in *My Four Years In Germany,* a war picture which proved to be a great box office sensation.

JOAN DAVIS

Born: June 29, 1907. Died: May 23, 1961. Birthplace: St. Paul, Minnesota. Height: 5′5″. Weight: 120 lbs. Red-brown hair and green eyes. At the age of three she was singing and speaking pieces in church entertainments. At seven she was doing a fourteen minute comedy single on the Pantages Circuit entitled *Toy Comedienne*, her parents and a tutor accompanying her. On March 12, 1931 her manager teamed her with Serenus (Si) Wills and they toured as Wills and Davis until March 1936. On August 13, 1931 they were married and two years later a daughter, Beverly, was born.

In March of 1936 they decided to leave the stage and make their future in motion pictures in order to give Beverly a permanent home.

Joan Davis made her first screen appearance in 1934 when she started as a hillbilly in a short, *Way Up Thar*, directed by Max Sennett. Her picture credits include: *The Holy Terror; On the Avenue; Time Out For Romance; The Great Hospital Mystery; Life Begins In College; Wake Up And Live; Thin Ice; Sally, Irene And Mary; Angel's Holiday; Sing Along And Be Happy; Love And Hisses; Josette; My Lucky Star; Just Around The Corner; Hold That Coed;* etc.

Her childhood stage experience combined with her motion picture career developed her into a fine comedienne. She will always be remembered for her TV series "I Married Joan" which ran in the 1950's.

She Gets Her Man, (Universal Studios, 1945). These two laugh-getters, Joan Davis and Leon Errol, were united in the zany comedy-whodunit. Joan Davis starred in this Universal Production with strong support from William Gargan, Vivian Austin, Virginia Sale and Milburn Stone. The combination of comedy and murder mystery proved to be successful.

George White's Scandals,
(R.K.O. Radio Picture, 1945).

Make Mine Laughs,
(R.K.O. Radio Picture, 1949).
A team of Haley and Davis continued their successful comedy antics with the box offices all reporting thriving business. She had appeared in motion pictures with Alice Faye, Don Ameche, Tyrone Power, Eddie Cantor, Bing Crosby, Milton Berle, Sonja Henie and Dick Powell.

Show Business, (R.K.O. Radio Pictures).

This film was one of the most famous to come out of the R.K.O. Studios. Eddie Cantor starred with Joan Davis. In this scene from the picture we see a story segment on Cleopatra as played by Joan Davis with Eddie Cantor as Antony. Joseph Vitale portrayed Caesar in this hilarious travesty on history.

I Married Joan, (TV show, 1950's).
In this series Jim Backus played Judge Stevens and Joan Davis played his perplexing wife.

JAMES DEAN

Born: February 8, 1931, Marion, Indiana. Died: September 30, 1955. His father Winton, was a dental technician and his mother Mildred Wilson died when he was nine.

Jimmy went to live with his aunt and uncle, the Marcus Winslows on their prosperous farm in Fairmount, Indiana. Well cared for, he was given a good education and after two college years, he majored in theater and went to Broadway for his try at stage fame. He was successful in getting a good part in a New York Stage Play, *The Immoralist*. Elia Kazan, the great motion picture director, caught his play, was impressed with his work and signed him up for motion pictures.

He made his screen debut in *East Of Eden* which proved to be an instant success, and hurtled him into motion picture immortality. His next film was *Rebel Without A Cause* and this picture too was very successful. His final film was *Giant*, a George Stevens Production, taken from the novel by Edna Ferber. At the height of his career he bought a $7,000 Porsche Speedster. Driving to Northern California he collided with another car and died shortly thereafter.

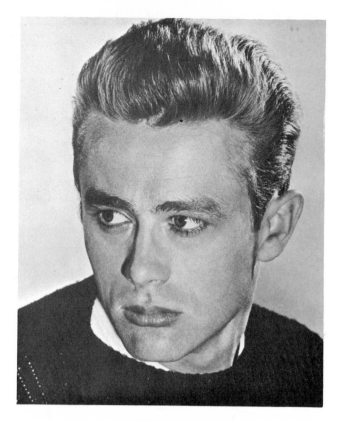

JAMES DEAN

The Immoralist, (New York Stage Play, 1954). He played the blackmailing Arab in this play and won an award as the most promising newcomer of 1954. This play was to serve as a stepping stone to his tragically short film career.

The Immoralist, (New York Stage Play, 1954). In this scene, James Dean is practicing his wiles and charm on Geraldine Page. One of the great directors of the screen, Elia Kazan, saw him in this play, recognized his ability and signed him up to a screen contract.

Rebel Without A Cause, (Warner Bros. Picture Inc. 1955).
Produced by David Weisbart and directed by Nicholas Ray.
James Dean, Natalie Wood and Sal Mineo were costarred in
the teenage picture. This film carried on the pattern of James
Dean's great success. He was a serious, earnest actor, studying
to become a director, totally unaware that this was never to
be. In this film Jim Backus and Ann Doran played his parents.

East of Eden, (Warner Bros. Picture).
This story was from the book by John
Steinbeck. Elia Kazan produced and
directed this production. This picture
starred James Dean, Julie Harris and
Raymond Massey.

Giant, (Warner Bros. Production, 1956).
Produced by George Stevens. James Dean played Jett Rink,
a violent ranch hand. He was costarred with Elizabeth Taylor
and Rock Hudson. Included in the cast were Carroll Baker,
Jane Withers, Chill Wills and Mercedes McCambridge.

CECIL BLOUNT DeMILLE

Born: August 12, 1881. Died: January 21, 1959. Birthplace: Ashfield, Mass.

This film figure was the co-founder with Samuel Goldwyn and Jesse L. Lasky in 1913 of the Jesse L. Lasky Feature Play Company for which he was director-general. The company merged in 1918 to become the Famous Player-Laskey, and in 1927 to become the present Paramount Picture Corp. His producing career ran from 1913, beginning with the *Squaw Man*, and ending with the second version of *The Ten Commandments*. By 1956 he had produced and directed seventy pictures.

Included among his screen credits are: *Male And Female, The Virginian, The Cheat, The Trail Of The Lonesome Pine, Joan The Woman, The Affairs Of Anatol, Manslaughter, Adam's Rib, The Volga Boatman, The King Of Kings, The Sign Of The Cross, Cleopatra, The Crusades, The Plainsman, The Buccaneer, Union Pacific, Northwest Mounted Police, Reap The Wild Wind, The Story Of Dr. Wassell, Unconquered, Samson And Delilah, The Greatest Show On Earth. The Ten Commandments* was his last film.

Cecil B. DeMille was called the master of the colossal and spectacular. He was a dramatist with a purpose. To DeMille, sound dramatic construction was the essential framework of a film. No director ever had a cannier sense of how to fill the screen and the eye of the beholder with spectacular action.

As a producer and as a director, he was to invent and incorporate many new innovations. Hundreds of thousands of dollars were devoted to research in his films.

Squaw Man, (Jesse Lasky Feature Play Company, 1913).

This picture was made in the original barn at Selma and Vine and in the Hollywood Hills. Dustin Farnum was recruited from the New York Stage and played the title role. A legend about Dustin Farnum claims he was offered stock in the Lasky Company in lieu of salary. He was supposed to have indignantly refused, thereby throwing away several million dollars. Included in the supporting cast were: Monroe Salisbury, Billy Elmer and Winifred Kingston.

The Ten Commandments, (Paramount, 1923).

This film is considered the very greatest of all the DeMille spectaculars for the silent era. In this famous action photo we see the film veteran, Theodore Roberts playing the part of Moses as he leads his people across the Red Sea. Cecil B. DeMille is now rated as the greatest showman of his time. More than three billion film goers have seen the pictures he has produced and directed in the past forty years.

King Of Kings, (Paramount, 1927).

This biblical spectacle was conceived and adapted for the screen by Jeanie MacPherson. H. B. Warner played the Christ figure and Sam De Grasse and Theodore Kosloff were in the supporting cast. In this scene we see Jesus as the crowd stones Magdalene, the fallen woman, muttering his famous words, "Let he who is without sin among you, cast the first stone."

Cleopatra, (Paramount, 1934).

In this DeMille spectacular, Claudette Colbert was costarred with Warren William and Henry Wilcoxon. Included in the supporting cast were: Ian Keith, Joseph Schildkraut, C. Aubrey Smith and Gertrude Michael. There had been many versions of Cleopatra before DeMille's version appeared on the screen, but his was acknowledged to be the greatest of them all. The lavish sets, the stunning costuming and the use of the top flight players of the thirties all combined to make this film one of his most outstanding pictures.

Samson And Delilah, (Paramount, 1949).

Victor Mature enacted the part of Samson and Hedy Lamarr played the part of Delilah with a magnificent supporting cast including: Angela Lansbury, George Sanders and Henry Wilcoxon. In this action photo from the picture Delilah attempts to learn the secret of Samson's strength and busies herself towards that objective with music and considerable feminine allure.

RICHARD DIX

Born: 1894, St. Paul, Minnesota. Died: 1949. Height: 6'. Weight: 180 lbs. Dark hair and brown eyes. Richard Dix attended the University of Minnesota for one year where he studied to be a surgeon, but left to take a position in a bank.

He soon tired of this and tried his hand in an architect's office. While working there he attended an evening high school course in dramatics, which led to a job with a local stock company. He moved to New York where he played in several stock companies. After a year in New York, Richard decided to go west. In Los Angeles he became leading man for the Morosco Stock Company in which he became a big success.

It was but natural that he should go into pictures after his success on the stage. In his first film, *Not Guilty*, produced by Joseph M. Schenck, he proved himself, and signed a long term contract with Paramount Studios.

His Paramount screen credits were: *The Vanishing American, Woman Handled, The Quarterback, Paradise For Two, Red Skin, Nothing But The Truth, The Wheel Of Life* and others.

Later, Dix was signed up by R.K.O.-Radio Pictures and starred in *Seven Keys To Baldpate, Loving The Ladies, Shooting Straight, The Public Defender, Cimarron, Donovan's Kid, Secret Service, The Lost Squadron, Roar Of The Dragon, The Great Jasper, No Marriage Ties,* and *I Won A Medal, Stingaree,* (M.G.M., 1934); *West Of The Pecos*, R.K.O., 1935; *Twelve Crowded Hours*, R.K.O. 1939; *Reno, Man Of Conquest, The Marines Fly High*, 20th Century Fox, 1940; *American Empire*, Paramount, 1942, and *Buckskin Frontier*, United Artists, 1943.

He reached his greatest pinnacle of his acting career when he played the part of Yancey Graves,

RICHARD DIX

the itinerant printer in the story of the early history of Oklahoma in *Cimarron*. For his part of Yancey Graves in *Cimarron* he will be remembered through the ages as one of our very finest immortals of the film.

The Ten Commandments, (Paramount, 1923). Cecil B. De Mille. In his version of this biblical picture, Richard Dix costarred with Rod La Rocque and Edythe Chapman. He was an inveterate pipe smoker who had thousands of pipes presented to him by admiring fans.

The Vanishing American, (Paramount, 1925).
Richard Dix was costarred with Lois Wilson in this story of the American Indians with all the injustices, privations, sufferings and their virtual extinction by the white man. In this scene we see Richard Dix and Lois Wilson playing with the little Indian, Nasja.

Quicksands, (Paramount, 1928).
Helene Chadwick played the feminine lead in this film. Richard Dix traced his ancestry back to the Pilgrim Days, for John Brimmer and Elizabeth Manchester, sweethearts on the Mayflower, bound from England to New England, later married and became the head of Dix's family.

Cimarron, (R.K.O.-Radio Picture, 1931).
This picture is considered to be Richard Dix's greatest. Irene Dunne played the feminine lead. William Collier Jr. immortalized himself in the part of the young bandit in this picture.

Man Of Conquest, (Republic Production, 1939).
In this biographical film on the life of Sam Houston, Richard Dix played the title role. In this tense action scene he is shown in a hand-to-hand fight with a Creek Warrior. This picture was Republic's spectacular of 1939.

LOUISE DRESSER

Born: October 5, 1882. Died: April 24, 1965.

She ran away from home at the age of 16 and worked her way into the theatrical world to become a great success on the stage and in vaudeville.

Her screen credits include: *Goose Woman*, Universal; *Mother Knows Best, Air Circus*, Fox; *Padlocked*, Paramount, 1929; *Not Quite Decent*, Fox; *Madonna Of Avenue A; Mad World*, M.G.M., 1930; *Three Sisters*, Fox; *Mammy*, Warner Bros.; *Caught*, Paramount; *State Fair, Doctor Bull, Song Of The Eagle, Cradle Song.*

LOUISE DRESSER

The Eagle, (1925).
The immortal Rudolph Valentino played the title role and Louise Dresser played the part of Catherine The Great of Russia in this action-romance of the Russian Steppes. Her characterization in this film places her forevermore among our great screen immortals.

Caught, (Paramount, 1931).
In this Western she costarred with Richard Arlen and played the part of a dance hall Madam. Her outstanding work in this production brought her a long term contract with the Paramount Studios.

Stepping Sisters, (Fox, 1932).
This picture costarred a trio of character women who were to make their individual fame on the screen. In this scene we see Minna Gambell, Louise Dresser and Jobyna Howard. Louise Dresser was married to Jack Gardner until Jack's death in 1950, ending their forty-two year marriage.

State Fair, (Fox, 1935).
The immortal Will Rogers costarred with Louise Dresser in this film of the big once-a-year doings of an agricultural state. Louise Dresser proved to be a perfect foil for Rogers' homespun style of performance and acting. *State Fair* according to many critics, was her greatest film.

During the first presentation of the Academy Awards Louise Dresser received a citation of merit.

Maid Of Salem, (Paramount, 1936).
Claudette Colbert and Fred MacMurray starred in this Frank Lloyd Production and Louise Dresser played a very strong character role. This picture had a great cast including: Harvey Stephens, Gail Sondergaard, Edward Ellis, E. E. Clive, Mary Treen, Bonita Granville, Virginia Weidler and Bennie Bartlette.

ROBERT DONAT

ROBERT DONAT

Born: March 18, 1905, Manchester, England. Died: 1958. Dark hair and brown eyes.

He played his first stage part in Birmingham, England in 1921. He did leads in touring companies and in London; he was also a stage manager and assistant director. He was placed under contract to London Film Production in 1932 by Alexander Korda.

His first screen credits were: *Men Of Tomorrow, That Night In London, Cash*; in 1933: *The Private Life Of Henry The Eighth*; in 1934: *The Count Of Monte Cristo*, (United Artists.)

He made his Hollywood debut in 1934, performed thereafter in many British Productions and Pictures of American distribution made in England. He won the Academy Award of 1939 in *Good-bye, Mr. Chips*, (M.G.M.). He was voted one of the best ten money-making British stars, Motion Pictures Hall-of-Fame Polls of 1942-43-46.

The Count Of Monte Cristo, (United Artists, 1934).
An Alexander Dumas novel. Robert Donat costarred with Elissa Landi and Sidney Blackmer. In this picture Robert Donat played the title role and Sidney Blackmer played the part of the heavy with his usual strong characterization. This picture was among the very first of Donat's films.

The Ghost Goes West,
(United Artists, 1936).
An Alexander Korda Production.
This picture was made in England.
Eugene Pallette played comedy re-
lief in this film.

Knight Without Armor, (United Artists, 1937).
Alexander Korda Production. In this tale of European intrigue Marlene Dietrich starred with Robert
Donat. *Knight Without Armor* was filmed and
adapted from the book of James Hilton.

Good-bye, Mr. Chips, (M.G.M., 1939).
Greer Garson, Robert Donat and John Mills had the
leading roles in this British production of the James
Hilton novel.

The Inn Of The Sixth Happiness,
(1958).
Robert Donat with Ingrid Bergman
and Curt Jurgens. This picture was
to ring down the final curtain on
Robert Donat's unbroken pattern of
success. Immediately after working
in this picture he died from a complication of respiratory ailments.

103

PAUL DOUGLAS

Born: April 11, 1907. Died: 1959. Birthplace: Philadelphia, Pennsylvania.

Education at Yale University. He was in school and Little Theater Dramatics. He was a radio announcer, sports narrator and writer for eleven years with some New York stage work.

His screen credits include: *Letters To Three Wives, It Happens Every Spring, Panic In The Streets, Fourteen Hours, Guy Who Came Back, Angels In The Outfield, When In Rome, Clash By Night, Never Wave At A Wac,* and *Executive Suite.*

His premature death in 1959 at the age of fifty-two was a great loss to the motion picture industry. His inspired performance in *Executive Suite* definitely places him among the great immortals of the screen.

It Happens Every Spring, (Fox, 1949).
Ray Milland, Jean Peters and Paul Douglas were costarred in this baseball comedy. Ray Milland played a professor who invented a solution which enabled a baseball to avoid the bat.

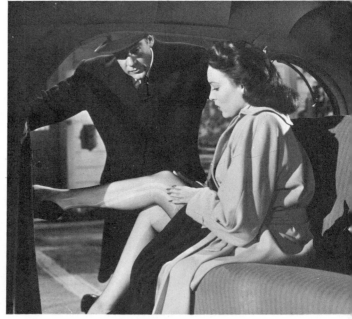

A Letter To Three Wives, (Fox, 1949).
This picture was Paul Douglas' first major film. The "Three Wives" concerned were played by Jeanne Crain, Linda Darnell and Ann Sothern, costarring Kirk Douglas, Paul Douglas, Barbara Lawrence and Jeffrey Lynn. Thelma Ritter was outstanding in her performance as a maid.

Clash By Night, (R.K.O., 1952).
Paul Douglas and Robert Ryan played the male leads, costarred with Barbara Stanwyck. This picture also had Marilyn Monroe in a supporting role. In this action scene we see Paul Douglas and Robert Ryan locked in conflict over the love of one woman, Barbara Stanwyck.

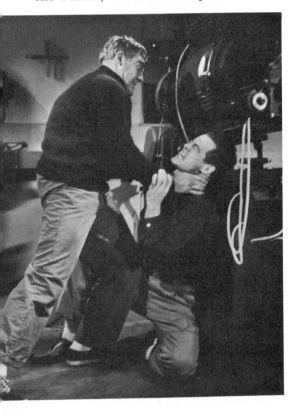

The Big Lift, (Fox, 1950).
Montgomery Clift and Paul Douglas costarred in the story of the famous air operation by the United States to bring food and supplies to the German populace.

Executive Suite, (M.G.M., 1954).
This film was a spectacular which M.G.M. produced in 1954. The story action revealed the power struggle inside a mammoth corporation. Fredric March William Holden, Barbara Stanwyck, and June Allyson starred. The distinguished cast included Paul Douglas, Walter Pidgeon, Shelley Winters and Louis Calhern.

DOUGLAS FAIRBANKS

Born: May 23, 1884, Denver, Colorado. Died: 1939. Height: 5'10". Weight: 165 lbs. Dark brown hair and eyes.

Educated in the Denver City Schools and the Colorado School Of Mines. The family went to New York City in 1901 and Douglas Fairbanks secured his first stage experience with Fredrick Warde.

His stage experience was in Shakespearian plays in New York, in *Mrs. Jack* supporting Alice Fisher, *The Pit, The Gentleman From Mississippi* and many others. He started his picture career with D. W. Griffith in 1914 and his early screen credits are as follows: *The Lamb, Double Trouble, Reggie Mixes In, The Americano, The Good Bad Man, Manhattan Madness.* Under contract for Famous Players he appeared in: *In Again Out Again, Wild And Woolly, Down To Earth* and *The Man From The Painted Past.*

In the latter part of his career he created many of his greatest films such as: *The Mark Of Zorro, The Mollycoddle, The Nut, Robin Hood, The Thief Of Bagdad, Don Q, The Son Of Zorro, The Black Pirate, The Gaucho, The Iron Mask, Taming Of The Shrew, Reaching For The Moon, Around The World In Eighty Minutes, Mr. Robinson Crusoe* and many, many others.

DOUGLAS FAIRBANKS

His Majesty, The American, (United Artists, 1919).

This film was the first one released by United Artists and 1919 was also the year the company was organized. Douglas Fairbanks was one of the owner-founders of United Artists. He was one of the screen's first and greatest of the swash buckling heroes whose astounding feats of daring-do have been imitated but never equalled. He braves danger with a smile and a strategically-placed forefinger in this scene.

The Three Musketeers, (United Artists, 1920).
Douglas Fairbanks played the part of D'Artagnan in this famous Dumas French Royalty classic. In this scene Douglas Fairbanks did some strenuous climbing to reach the eager lips of Marguerite Da La Motte.

Robin Hood, (United Artists, 1922).
This film showed Douglas Fairbanks at the very height of his career as he portrayed the title role of Robin Hood. His matchless coordination and exceptionally fast reflexes provided wonderful entertainment as he roamed through the English countryside taking from the rich and giving to the poor.

The Thief Of Bagdad, (United Artists, 1924).
In this picture Fairbanks plays the title role of a notorious thief who reforms for the sake of his beloved princess. Julianne Johnston played the part of the princess. This scene shows the two of them on the "magic carpet" as they fly over the minarets of Arabia.

The Taming Of The Shrew, (United Artists, 1929).
In this famous Shakespearian comedy Mary Pickford and Douglas Fairbanks costarred. This was the first and the last time that the King and the Queen of the silent screen appeared together in a film.

DUSTIN FARNUM

DUSTIN FARNUM

Born: 1876, Hampton Beach, New Hampshire. Died: 1929, Los Angeles, California. Height: 5'11". Weight: 170 lbs. Brown hair and brown eyes.

While attending school at Lockport, Maine, he made his first professional stage appearance in a play called *The Hidden Hand*. On the completion of his education he joined up with the Ethel Tucker Repertory Company; then worked with Marguerite Mather for 18 months following which he played two years with Chauncey Olcott. As he became established and gained recognition, he was given strong parts in the great dramas of the day, and he appeared in *Arizona*. He played the title role of *The Virginian* and worked for three seasons at the Herald Square Theater in New York City. Then, in 1909 he played in *The Squaw Man* at the Hackett Theater in New York, and in the latter part of 1909 he worked in *Cameo Kirby*. His entire life was to be changed by his stage appearance in *The Squaw Man*. About this time Cecil B. De Mille and Jesse Lasky had decided to start a motion picture company, and at the right time and the right place they hired Dustin Farnum to do the screen version of *The Squaw Man*. From then on he worked in the motion pictures throughout the rest of his career. His screen credits include in 1913 — *The Squaw Man*; in 1915 — *Cameo Kirby*; in 1916 — *Captain Courtesy* and *The Iron Strain*; in 1917 — *David Garrick* and *The Scarlet Pimpernell*; in 1918 — *The Spy And North* of 53; in 1919 — *Light Of The Western Stars, A Man's Fight, A Man In The Open*; in 1920 — *The Corsican Brothers*; in 1921 *Big Happiness And The Primal Law*; in 1922 — *Strange Idols, Iron To Gold, The Devil Within* and *The Yosemite Trail*; in 1924 — *Kentucky Days*; and in 1926 — *The Flaming Frontier* and many, many others.

The Squaw Man, (Lasky Feature Company, 1913). Dustin Farnum had starred in Edwin Milton Royle's great stage success *The Squaw Man*, so Laskey and De Mille knew that Farnum would be ideal for the screen role. In 1913 the entire company went to Los Angeles from New York City. In a suburb of Hollywood they rented an old barn for $100 per week and started shooting, finishing *The Squaw Man* in the space of 3 weeks.

The Squaw Man, (Lasky Feature Company, 1913).

In this scene of the film we see Dustin Farnum in his part of *The Squaw Man*. Just to the left was Al Reno, a noted character actor of the day, and the man under the gun, playing one of the heavies of the picture, was Billy Elmer, a Western actor. Cecil B. DeMille's first picture had cost $20,000 and eventually grossed $400,000, and sales of *The Squaw Man* returned to the Lasky Company almost twice the cash value of their original capital.

Davy Crockett, (Paramount, 1916).

Dustin Farnum played the title role of this film in the early days of the Paramount era. In the annals of screen history William Farnum, Dustin's brother, also became a noted screen star. Most of his early work was for William Fox, and he became a Western star.

The Virginian, (Paramount, 1923) (De Mille).

In 1907 Farnum had played the part of the *The Virginian* for three seasons in New York City, and in his screen career he played the part for Cecil B. De Mille. The motion picture screen took a great succession of famous stage plays and made screen adaptations of them. It was not until later that the writers were forced to come up with original scripts, new ideas and fresh situations.

Film Company Of The Early Days—*Call Of The North*, (Paramount, 1921).

This photo shows an illustrious group of early film pioneers. Reading from left to right are Charlie Ross, Theodore Roberts, James Neill, Max Figman, Dustin Farnum, Stewart Edward White and Robert Edeson, with Oscar Apfel and Cecil B. De Mille seated.

MARIE DRESSLER

Born: November 9, 1869, Coburg, Ontario, Canada. Height: 5'7".
Weight: 150 lbs. Red hair and green eyes.

Made her first public appearance as Cupid on a pedestal at the
age of five in a church theatrical performance. She was laughed at
in a theatrical show as an amateur in Lindsay, Canada, when she
was fourteen. In her forty-five years of circus, vaudeville, stage and
screen experience she included everything from chorus to stardom.
She made her screen debut in *Tillie's Punctured Romance* opposite
Charlie Chaplin.

Her screen credits were the following M.G.M. Productions: *Calla-
hans And The Murphys, Bringing Up Father, The Patsy, Anna
Christie* and *Hollywood Review.* Then for outside studios: *Divine
Lady, Joy Girl, Vagabond Lover* and for R.K.O. *Caught Short.* In
1932 she returned to M.G.M. in *Emma, Politics, Reducing* and *Prosperity.* In the year of 1933 on the M.G.M. lot she did *Tugboat Annie,
Dinner At Eight,* and *Christopher Bean.*

It would be a very difficult decision to select from her many great
inspired performances the one which placed her among the screen
immortals. But the role of the Waterfront Hag in *Anna Christie* is
probably her most unforgettable part.

Tillie's Punctured Romance,
(Keystone Comedy, 1914).
(Directed by Mack Sennett).

This film starred Mabel Normand, Charles Chaplin and Marie Dressler. Fresh from her triumphs on the New York Musical Comedy Stage she fitted in this picture and proved perfect foil for Charlie Chaplin's funny situations. It was a terrible irony that she was not to stay with the Mack Sennett group and lend her acting genius to their comedies.

Anna Christie, (M.G.M., 1930).
Greta Garbo starred in this film. Marie Dressler was in the supporting cast with George Marion. Marie Dressler played "Marthy," a saloon habitue of the waterfront. She immortalized this part and many authorities believe she dominated and took most of the honors in this film.

Min And Bill, (M.G.M., 1939).
Wallace Beery costarred with Marie Dressler and they turned out an inspired performance as the two earthy characters of this sea story. This picture burst like a bomb shell upon the theaters all over the nation and was one of the biggest box office smash hits of all time for M.G.M.

Christopher Bean, (M.G.M., 1933).

In this picture Marie was costarred with the famous Lionel Barrymore and together they created their theatrical magic and came up with a truly sensitive and fine film. Her performance was that of a house servant who always looked for poor large families so that she could feel a part of those large families instead of just a servant. They were supported by some of the very best contract players on the M.G.M. list including: Beulah Bondi, H. B. Warner and Jean Hersholt.

Dinner At Eight, (M.G.M., 1934). This film had a magnificent cast consisting of practically all of the theatrical personalities on the M.G.M. lot at that time such as: John Barrymore, Wallace Beery, Jean Harlow, and Lionel Barrymore. This picture was magnificently directed by George Cukor and was one of the greatest classics from 1934.

WILLIAM C. FIELDS

WILLIAM C. FIELDS

Born: February 10, 1879, Philadelphia, Penn. Died: 1946. Height: 5'8". Weight: 160 lbs. His career covered the stage, vaudeville, musical comedy, radio and motion pictures

His screen credits include: *That Royal Girl, It's The Old Army Game, Two Flaming Youths, Tillie's Punctured Romance* (the second version), *Fools For Luck* (Paramount), *Sally Of the Sawdust;* in 1933 — *If I Had A Million, International House* and *Paramount Short Features; David Copperfield* (M.G.M. 1935); *The Bank Dick* (Universal 1940); *Never Give The Sucker An Even Break* (Universal 1941).

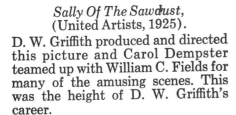

Sally Of The Sawdust, (United Artists, 1925).
D. W. Griffith produced and directed this picture and Carol Dempster teamed up with William C. Fields for many of the amusing scenes. This was the height of D. W. Griffith's career.

Tillie's Punctured Romance, (Paramount, 1927).

In this second version of this film, Louise Fazenda played the part of Tillie and Chester Conklin, a veteran of the Old Mack Sennett Comedy days, doubled up with W. C. Fields to supply the foils for the many comic situations which were required to puncture Tillie's romance.

The Bank Dick, (Universal, 1940).
Fresh from his many successes in radio, Fields was put under contract at the Universal Studios and was given Carte Blanche to concoct and invent his many comedy routines. In this scene, Richard Purcell and W. C. Fields show one of the situations.

Never Give A Sucker An Even Break, (Universal, 1941).
In this film he was costarred with Gloria Jean, Susan Miller, Leon Errol, Butch and Buddy and Franklin Pangborn.

David Copperfield, (M.G.M., 1935).
This picture was a big spectacular and in this old Dickens' Classic they recruited practically everybody on the M.G.M. lot. But W. C. Fields with his characterization walked off with all the comedy honors in spite of some of the finest competition among his many contemporaries.

BARRY FITZGERALD

Born: 1888 in Dublin, Ireland. Died: 1961. Height: 5′9″. Weight: 130 lbs. Gray hair and brown eyes.

Barry Fitzgerald started out in life as a junior clerk in the board of trade, but his ambitions were with the theater and the drama, and so at night he served his apprenticeship to the Abbey Theater and learned the acting craft in a professional manner. Sean O'Casey wrote *The Silver Tassle* and Barry became a full-fledged stage star. He came to Hollywood from Ireland in 1937 and became one of the finest supporting actors. He was in great demand and did several superb supporting roles which quickly elevated him to stardom. His screen credits include: *Plough And The Stars, Ebb Tide, Bringing Up Baby, Pacific Liner, Dawn Patrol, Four Men And A Prayer, Saint Strikes Back, Full Confession, The Long Voyage Home, The Sea Wolf, How Green Was My Valley, Two Tickets To London, None But The Lonely Heart, Duffy's Tavern, Welcome Stranger, The Naked City, Miss Tatlock's Millions, The Story Of Seabiscuit, Top O' The Morning, Union Station, Silver City, The Quiet Man, Tonight's The Night, The Catered Affair*, and many others.

Barry Fitzgerald came out of virtual retirement to costar in the English film, *Broth Of A Boy*. He was brought to Hollywood to do a supporting role in that immortal story of the Irish Rebellion, *The Plough And The Stars*. In Hollywood he stayed, and the rich Irish brogue of Barry Fitzgerald quickly made him a great favorite in American films. His greatest role was the kindly old priest in *Going My Way*, in which he costarred with Bing Crosby. He won the Oscar for his role in this picture as the best supporting actor for 1944, and in this part all his loyal fans will remember him. His passing left a void that no other actor can ever fill. He richly deserves the honor of being one of the screen's great immortals.

Going My Way, (Paramount, 1944).

After his arrival in Hollywood and at the conclusion of his supporting role in *The Plough And The Stars,* Barry Fitzgerald played in several superb supporting roles in the following pictures: *Ebb Tide, Four Men And A Prayer, The Dawn Patrol,* and *Bringing Up Baby.* In the year of 1944 he costarred in this picture. Together, he and Bing Crosby created a magic chemistry which brought forth an inspired performance from the both of them and won for them both the coveted Oscar. Bing Crosby's Oscar was given to him for the best male star of 1944, and Barry Fitzgerald's Oscar was for the best supporting star of 1944.

Easy Come, Easy Go, (Paramount, 1946).

After an actor wins an Oscar, it is customary for his salary to skyrocket and also for said actor to become in great demand. Barry Fitzgerald was no exception. In this scene we see him in the center and to the right of him is his brother, Arthur Shields, who also came to Hollywood and gained fame as an Irish actor with the full Irish brogue.

The Sainted Sisters,
(Paramount, 1948).

In the dual roles Veronica Lake and Joan Caulfield were costarred with Barry Fitzgerald in this story of a Western town at the turn of the century. The title of the story was misleading, as these particular sisters were anything but saintly. The entire plot consisted of the sisters' many attempts at fleecing Barry Fitzgerald out of his fortune, and this comedy provided a very good vehicle for Barry Fitzgerald's particular style of humor.

Top O' The Morning,
(Paramount, 1949).

Once again Bing Crosby and Barry Fitzgerald were costarred with Ann Blyth and Hume Cronyn. Prior to this picture Fitzgerald had worked with Crosby in 1947 in a picture called *Welcome Stranger*. In this scene from *Top O' The Morning* we see Bing Crosby, Barry Fitzgerald and Hume Cronyn having a bit of an argument. It was no happenstance that a goodly portion of the pictures in which Fitzgerald played his supporting roles, used Irish locales.

The Quiet Man, (Republic, 1952).

Under the misleading title of *The Quiet Man*, John Wayne in the title role, costarred with Maureen O'Hara, Victor McLaglen and Barry Fitzgerald. In this scene Barry Fitzgerald, as the marriage broker, asks Victor McLaglen for his sister's (Maureen O'Hara) hand in marriage in behalf of John Wayne.

ERROL FLYNN

Born: June 20, 1909. Died: 1959. Birthplace: North Ireland. Height: 6′2″. Brown hair and brown eyes. Educated in England and France.

Given to a life of adventure and excitement he sailed to England, made the rounds of producers' offices and found for himself a place as an actor on the English stage. He played several excellent roles which brought him to the attention of motion picture producers in England. Irving Asher, head of the Warner Bros. Studios in England made a screen test of him and brought it to Hollywood to show to the chiefs of production there.

The result was a contract for Flynn, who arrived in due time in Hollywood, to be more or less swallowed up in the great swarm of newcomers struggling for the chance on the American screen. He did, however, appear in two pictures, once as a returning husband who fought and was killed in *The Case Of The Curious Bride* and again, briefly, in *Don't Bet On Blondes*.

He married Lili Damita, a French actress, less than six months after he met her on ship board on his journey to America. That honeymoon was interrupted by his call to the studio to make tests for *Captain Blood*. The competition for the role was keen. *Captain Blood* was to be one of the most important pictures of the New Year. But there was an indefinable something that Flynn brought to those tests that no other actor seemed to have. His assurance, his ease in the swashbuckling, danger-loving characterization of Sabatini's hero, his background, his own adventurous life, were all caught by the camera. An "unknown" fitted the part of *Captain Blood* as few men have ever fitted a role on the screen before.

ERROL FLYNN

His screen credits include: *Captain Blood, Green Light, Prince And The Pauper, Dodge City, Charge Of The Light Brigade, Adventures Of Robin Hood, The Sea Hawk, They Died With Their Boots On* and many many others.

The Case Of The Curious Bride, (Warner Bros. Production, 1935). This is the first American picture in which Errol Flynn performed. His leading lady was Margaret Lindsay. The picture following this one was *Don't Bet On Blondes*.

118

Captain Blood, (Warner Bros. Production, 1935).
This picture was to catapult him into fame and fortune and was to be the first of many a great spectacular in which he was to star for Warner Bros. Olivia DeHavilland played a very sensitive, moving performance as his leading woman.

The Dawn Patrol, (Warner Bros., 1938).
Errol Flynn was costarred with Basil Rathbone, David Niven and Donald Crisp. He was now at the height of his fame and the role of a devil-may-care, roistering war aviator suited his acting talents and projected his personality to the many thousands of loyal fans who made every Flynn picture a smashing success at the box office.

Adventures Of Robin Hood, (Warner Bros. Technicolor Production, 1938).
Errol Flynn of course played Robin Hood with that grand veteran of stage and screen Basil Rathbone playing the part of the heavy and also his opponent in the dueling scenes. This film was recognized as one of the best versions of the Robin Hood story ever to be filmed.

The Sea Hawk,
(Warner Bros. First National Picture).
In this scene the galley slaves attempt to take over the ship and James Stephenson, Errol Flynn and Alan Hale prepared to fight to the death. He was to go on to many many more great films. His untimely death at the age of fifty was a great loss to the entire world but he had lived a full life with all of its pleasures.

PAULINE FREDERICK

Born: August 12, 1885, Boston, Massachusetts. Died: 1938.

Her stage experience began in *Roger's Brothers In Harvard* under the management of Ben Teal. Also, in the following dramas: *Joseph And His Brothers, Innocent, Samson,* and *When Knights Were Bold.* These great stage plays brought her unanimous critical acclaim and stardom on the stage before she achieved top billing on the screen. Her first starring picture was Famous Players' *The Eternal City.* For the next eight years she starred in such silent screen successes as: *Bella Donna, Zaza, La Tosca, Fedora, Resurrection, The Glorious Clementine, Slave Of Vanity,* and *The Lure Of Jade.*

Sam Goldwyn brought the lovely star to Hollywood for a series of films beginning with *Madame X* which she also played on the English stage for ten months. *The Paliser Case* and other films were followed by stage appearances in *Spring Cleaning* and *The Lady* with which she toured the major cities of this country and Australia for nine months.

On her return in 1932, Warner Brothers starred her in three talking pictures: *On Trial, Evidence,* and *The Sacred Flame.* Lubitsch directed her in *Three Women,* and Monogram starred her in *Self Defense.*

Then came her triumphal stage tour in the title role of *Elizabeth, The Queen* which was heralded as her greatest performance on either stage or screen.

She stayed in New York for several years doing stage plays very successfully, but homesickness for California brought her back to Hollywood where she was immediately signed by Fox for important mother roles in *Buccaneer* and *Ramona.* Her screen career as a topflight star covered twenty years of fine performances and dedicated work.

La Tosca, (Famous Players, 1918).
This film was among her first pictures, and her superb acting in this picture in all probability placed her well on the road to fame. She had been trained from childhood to be a singer and had a very fine mezzo-soprano voice, but her terrific acting ability soon placed the singing voice in abeyance.

Madame X, (Goldwyn, 1920).
Pauline Frederick played the title role with that great stage veteran, Sidney Ainsworth, and Casson Ferguson played the lawyer son. This film is recognized as one of Pauline Frederick's greatest performances.

Smouldering Fires, (Universal, 1924).
Pauline Frederick costarred with Laura LaPlante and Malcom McGregor. Despite her Boston background, Pauline Frederick admitted a love for Hawaiian music in preference to classical. She was a student of psychic phenomena and ancient religions, loved sun baths, cooking, sewing and knitting, and prefaced each role with an intensive sniffing spree to find the most expressive perfume equivalent of each character.

Wayward, (Paramount, 1932).
Pauline Frederick, Richard Arlen and Nancy Carroll costarred in this Paramount Production. Pauline Frederick was at her very best playing Mother roles to the new crop of stars clamoring at the gates of stardom. In the closing phases of her career Pauline Frederick lived in Beverly Hills with her two "white-haired babies"—her mother, Loretta Fisher Libby, and her aunt, Mrs. Carrie Fisher Pettingill.

Ramona, (Fox, 1936).
Loretta Young and Don Ameche starred with Pauline Frederick, Kent Taylor, John Carradine, Katherine DeMille, Jane Darwell, and J. Carrol Naish in the supporting roles. This picture was highly important since it was Fox's first attempt at full Technicolor in complete production.

CLARK GABLE

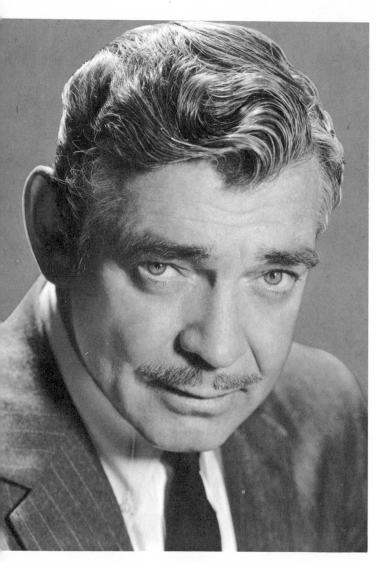

CLARK GABLE

Born: Cadiz, Ohio, February 1, 1901.

First jobs: tool dresser and stage call boy, toured with Jewell Players.

Stage Plays: *Lady Frederick, Madame X, Great Diamond Robbery, What Price Glory, Copperhead, Romeo And Juliet*, and *The Last Mile*.

Films: Among his very first on the M.G.M. lot was *Painted Desert*, 1931.

He started as a heavy in these early films but became one of the greatest personalities of the screen. As a leading man, both his comedy flair and his great sex appeal proved irresistible to the thousands of faithful feminine fans. His notable smash hits were: *Strange Interlude, The White Sister, Hell Divers, Polly Of The Circus, China Seas, Forsaking All Others, Mutiny On The Bounty, Call Of The Wild, Idiots Delight, Strange Cargo, Somewhere I'll Find You, Adventure, Command Decision, Hucksters, Homecoming, San Francisco, Any Number Can Play, Key To The City, To Please A Lady, Across The Wide Missouri, Lone Star, Never Let Me Go, Mogambo, Betrayed, Soldier Of Fortune, Tall Men, King And Four Queens, Band Of Angels, Teacher's Pet, But Not For Me, It Started In Naples.*

His last film, which contributed to his untimely death was *The Misfits*, in which he had the tragic Marilyn Monroe as his leading lady.

His war record shows he served in the U.S.A.F. with rank of major and went on several bombing missions.

He won the Academy Award for best performance in the year of 1934 for the film in which he costarred with Claudette Colbert, *It Happened One Night*, (Columbia). For this portrayal he is immortalized on the American Screen. But his great following will remember him forever in their hearts as Rhett Butler in *Gone With The Wind*. He died in Los Angeles, California on November 16, 1960.

The Painted Desert, (M.G.M., 1930).

Clark Gable played a Heavy in his first film. He was to play villains in a couple of other M.G.M. pictures and then become a romantic star. From this inauspicious beginning the career of Gable was to climb to the stars.

122

It Happened One Night, (Columbia, 1934).
In this picture Clark Gable won the Oscar for the best performance of 1934. Both he and Claudette Colbert were "lent" to Columbia from M.G.M.

Mutiny On The Bounty,
(M.G.M., 1935).

This film was Charles Laughton's American debut and as Captain Bligh he scored a smashing hit and soared to immediate stardom. But Clark Gable in his role as Fletcher Christian gave a very good account of himself in this film and added thousands of loyal fans to his faithful following. The love scenes with the Island Native Girl palpitated many a feminine heart.

Gone With The Wind, (Selznick, M.G.M., 1939).
In this immortal classic of the South, Clark Gable was cast as Rhett Butler.

The Misfits, 1960.
In this United Artists Production, Clark Gable was costarred with Marilyn Monroe and Montgomrey Clift. Working in high temperatures and doing strenuous and violent work undoubtedly contributed to his death. *The Misfits* was his final film.

125

Castle On The Hudson, (Warners, 1940).
Pat O'Brien, Ann Sheridan and John Garfield costarred in this typical Warner Brothers prison picture on life in Sing Sing. This picture was to be the pattern for John Garfield's success, for the role of the Tough Guy seemed to be so natural to him that he really lived the parts instead of just acting them.

JOHN GARFIELD

Born: March 4, 1913, New York City, New York. Died: May 21, 1952.

He was educated at the Angelo Patri School, New York. He attended the Ouspenskaya Dramatic School and then served an apprenticeship with Eva La Gallienne's Repertoire Company in New York. He was very successful on the New York stage in many dramatic productions which included: *Lost Boy, Counsellor-At-Law, Having A Wonderful Time* and *Golden Boy* with many, many others. His first picture was *Four Daughters* made in 1938. His screen credits include: *They Made Me A Criminal, Juarez, Dust Be My Destiny, Saturday's Children, The Sea Wolf, Air Force, Tortilla Flat, Thank Your Lucky Stars*. The latter phases of his career included *Hollywood Canteen, Nobody Lives Forever, Humoresque, Gentlemen's Agreement, Body And Soul, Force Of Evil, We Were Strangers, The Breaking Point*. His last picture was *He Ran All The Way*. In the film *Humoresque* he undoubtedly reached the pinnacle of his career.

Tortilla Flat, (M.G.M., 1942).
Spencer Tracy, Hedy Lamarr, John Garfield and Frank Morgan all costarred in John Steinbeck's great novel of Tortilla Flat. This story was based on Monterey's fishing industry with its assortment of weird characters who preyed upon the people of the town.

Dangerously They Live, (Warners, 1942). John Garfield, Nancy Coleman and Raymond Massey costarred with Moroni Olsen playing the supporting role. This particular type of picture proved to be very successful and the Warner Brothers evolved a success pattern and turned out many, many pictures involving prisons, gangsters, crooked cops, loose women and mob violence.

Humoresque, (Warners, 1946). John Garfield and Joan Crawford played the leads in this famous classic with J. Carrol Naish and Oscar Levant playing the supporting roles. John Garfield was superb as the struggling violinist, and Joan Crawford played the patroness of the arts who attempts to help and further his career. This role in *Humoresque* is considered to be John Garfield's greatest contribution to the screen.

Between Two Worlds, (Warners, 1944). John Garfield, Paul Henreid, Sydney Greenstreet, Eleanor Parker costarred in this picture. The plot of this film had a striking similarity to *Outward Bound*, and the fantasy elements had original situations and tense moments which made this picture a great box-office success.

HOOT GIBSON

HOOT GIBSON

Born: Tekamah, Nebraska, 1892. Height: 5′9″. Weight: 160 lbs. Light hair and blue eyes.

His first work was as a cowboy on various ranches and his cowboy life led him to many ranches in the Western States. He soon became one of the most daring riders in the West. In 1912 Gibson won the World's All-Around Cowboy Championship at the famous Pendleton round-up and with this noteworthy achievement for prestige he came to Hollywood. At that time Bronco Billy Anderson was the screen's headliner, Harry Pollard was a comedian, and Lois Weber an outstanding director as well as a star.

Gibson went from studio to studio doing trick riding for the more timorous stars. He is what is termed a "stunt" man and for risking his life every day, he was paid the magnificent sum of $25.00 a week. It was while doubling for a star that he was one day asked to play the role, the star having been injured in an automobile accident. He made good and from that time on has been acting in front of the camera. The greatest part of his career and the biggest majority of his pictures were associated with Universal Studios.

His screen credits include: *Smilin' Guns, Burning The Wind, King Of The Rodeo, Lariat Kid, Points West, The Winged Horseman, Courting Wild Cats, The Long Long Trail*, produced in 1929 at Universal. *Mounted Stranger, Roaring Ranch, Spurs, Trailing Trouble, Trigger Tricks*, (Universal 1930). *Clearing The Range, Gay Buckaroo, Hard Hombre, Local Badman, Spirit Of The West, Wild Horse, A Man's Land, The Boiling Point, Cowboy Counsellor*, were produced at Universal in 1931-32. In 1933 he worked for the Allied Artists and his pictures were *Boots Of Destiny, The Dude Bandit. The Fighting Parson* and many, many others.

Hoot Gibson was a true son of the Old West, a real western cowboy from many many years of actual experience and his western roles magnificently portrayed the true western spirit and customs of the old time cowboy.

Untitled Early Western, 1925
In this action scene Hoot Gibson punches his way out of a tight spot, and his companion in distress, wielding the chair on one of the villains, is Blanche Mahaffey, a very popular actress of that era. Blanche Mahaffey started her career as a bathing girl in the Hal Roach comedies and rose to become a very popular leading lady.

The Rawhide Kid, (Universal, 1927).

Hoot Gibson had formed his own company, had started this western series and was enjoying great success, especially from the boys of America of that era. His hobby in later years was flying. He acquired his pilot's license and was known as the "Flying Cowboy."

Galloping Fury, (Universal, 1927).

In this picture Hoot Gibson costarred with Sally Rand. Sally Rand at that time was playing feminine leads, and this was slightly before the era of the fan dance. Many of the feminine stars developed their acting talents and eventually learned to specialize in a certain type of film.

Points West, (Universal, 1929).

In this photo we see Hoot Gibson fixing himself a bacon supper. The simple, elementary methods used to prepare a western supper may not have appealed to the mature set, but the kids of that era thought this was the greatest stuff in the world.

Sunset Range, (First Division, 1935).

Hoot Gibson and Martha Sleeper costarred in this successful western film. Hoot Gibson's manner was genial and he had many friends. While shy in public, he had the ability of making acquaintances easily. He lived an exemplary life, and he was always the cowboy hero whom the boys adored, and their fan letters were the source of great interest and inspiration to him. Knowing how growing lads hero-worship, he selected his own stories with the utmost care, and undoubtedly owed much of his success and popularity to this vigilance.

Wolf Song, (Paramount, 1929).

In this Paramount Production she was costarred with Gary Cooper and Louis Wolheim. This picture was one of her early ones and showed great promise and the potential of her acting career. One of Lupe's deviations from her screen career was when Jimmy Durante persuaded her to costar with him in the great New York-Broadway Musical successes *Hot-Cha* and *Strike Me Pink*.

Cuban Love Song, (M.G.M., 1931).

Lawrence Tibbett, fresh from his great operatic successes, was placed under contract to M.G.M. and in this production was costarred with Lupe Velez. One of M.G.M.'s most famous directors, W. S. Van Dyke, lent his fine talents to the direction of this film.

LUPE VELEZ

Born: July 18, 1910, San Louis Potosi, Mexico. Died: 1956. Height: 5 feet. Weight: 115 lbs. Black hair and brown eyes.

Educated by Our Lady Of The Lake Convent, San Antonio, Texas. Richard Bennett, the veteran American stage actor, discovered Lupe in Mexico City when she played in *Rataplan*, a Mexican Musical Comedy, and he brought her to the United States. In Hollywood, she obtained her first screen work in Laurel and Hardy comedies for Hal Roach.

Her first important motion picture assignment was in a supporting role for Douglas Fairbanks in *The Gaucho*, and from then onward her success was assured. Her screen credits include: *Stand And Deliver, Wolf Song, Lady Of The Pavements, Where East Is East*, with Lon Chaney; *Tiger Rose, Hell's Harbor, The Storm,* Tolstoy's *Resurrection, The Squaw Man, The Cuban Love Song, East Is West, Hot Pepper, The Half-Naked Truth, The Broken Wing, Kongo*, and many, many others.

She was affectionately nicknamed "The Mexican Spitfire." Her volcanic Latin mannerisms and her volatile Spanish temperament attracted thousands upon thousands of faithful admirers and fans.

130

Resurrection, (Universal, 1931).

This film was based on a Russian novel by Count Leo Tolstoy and Universal even brought Count Tolstoy over to the United States for the express purpose of supervising the script, making sure of the proper Russian atmosphere, etc., etc. John Boles, a gifted American Singer, was costarred with Lupe Velez in this picture, and their combined talents made it one of the finer Universal Pictures.

The Broken Wing, (Paramount, 1932).

Two great Spanish personalities were merged to costar in this film. Leo Carrillo had a distinguished stage career, spent many years in vaudeville and was at the height of his career when he was teamed up with the "Mexican Spitfire."

Hot Pepper, (Fox, 1933).

It was a moot question as to whether "Hot Pepper" was a title role for Lupe Velez. She was costarred with Victor McLaglen, Edmund Lowe and El Brendel. In the latter part of her career she was signed up with R.K.O. and costarred with Leon Errol in a series which allowed her full projection of her vital personality. It was especially written for her and was called the "Mexican Spitfire" series.

131

JOHN GILBERT

Born: July 10, 1897. Died: 1936. Birthplace: Logan, Utah. Height: 5'11". Weight: 165 lbs. Brown hair and brown eyes.

He played his first role on the stage when he was a year old with Eddie Foy. He worked in various occupations but finally decided on acting. He told his Mother who sent his letters and pictures to Walter Edwards, Director for Thomas H. Ince, of the New York Motion Picture Corporation, in Inceville, Santa Monica, California.

He received word to come to the studio and while there met Herschel Mayall, an old friend of his father, who introduced him and helped him get started in pictures. Ince finally gave him a two year contract at thirty dollars a week for the first year and forty the second. In his first picture, *Princess Of The Dark* he costarred with Enid Bennett.

After many periods of hardship and lean times in the picture game he appeared in *Cameo Kirby* and was brought to the attention of Irving G. Thalberg, then a producer for Louis B. Mayer. He refused to sign a new contract with Fox and got a five year contract with the new Metro-Goldwyn-Mayer. He costarred in *He Who Gets Slapped, Wife Of The Centaur,* and *The Merry Widow.*

His greatest starring picture for M.G.M. was *The Big Parade.* He next starred in *La Boheme, Bordelys The Magnificent, Flesh And The Devil, The Show, Twelve Miles Out, Love, Man, Woman and Sin, The Snob, Fires Of Youth, The Cossacks, Thirst, A Woman Of Affairs, Redemption, Queen Christina* and many, many others. *The Big Parade* undoubtedly was his greatest picture.

JOHN GILBERT

Princess Of The Dark, (Ince Productions, 1917).
This was John Gilbert's first starring role and Enid Bennett played the feminine lead. But it was to be many years later before he was placed under contract to Metro-Goldwyn-Mayer.

132

The Big Parade,
(Metro-Goldwyn-Mayer Productions, 1925).
This picture was to be the turning point in John Gilbert's career; in this hit, success, fame and fortune came to him from this one great picture. In this scene we see Gilbert and O'Brien on the battlefield as Karl Dane expires.

Flesh And The Devil,
(Metro-Goldwyn-Mayer, 1927).
John Gilbert costarred with Greta Garbo and Marc McDermott; this dramatic scene shows McDermott passing the challenge to a duel of honor to John Gilbert with Greta Garbo portraying one of her earliest roles with M.G.M.

The Merry Widow,
(Metro-Goldwyn-Mayer, 1925).

The Cossacks, (Metro-Goldwyn-Mayer, 1928).
This film was a great change of pace in John Gilbert's acting career. He was costarred with Ernest Torrence.

Oh, Yeah, (R.K.O. Radio, 1930).
James Gleason was costarred with Zasu Pitts and Robert Armstrong in this comedy. This picture was among the very first of James Gleason's long career. Just prior to the time of working in this picture he had written the original play of *Oh, Yeah!*

JAMES GLEASON

Born: May 23, 1886, New York City. Died: April 12, 1959 in Woodland Hills, California.

James Gleason was small, gentle-mannered and cultured, but he was pegged for police parts. Perhaps it was because he could talk out of the side of his mouth!

His first appearance on stage was at the tender age of four months in the arms of his Mother, Mina Crolius, who was playing with his actor-father, William Gleason. He continued to play child parts on the stage. When he grew up, he enlisted in the United States Army and served during the Philippine insurrection. Upon his return to the United States, Gleason played stock, vaudeville and comedy on Broadway and then came to Hollywood with Irving Berlin to write a musical. Fresh from his great success of his plays *Is Zat So?*, *The Fall Guy* and *The Shannons Of Broadway*, he wrote short comedies and appeared in such feature pictures as *Oh Yeah, Her Man, Beyond Victory, A Free Soul, Suicide Fleet.*

His picture credits include: *Here Comes Mr. Jordan, The Yellow Cab Man, What Price Glory, The Story Of Will Rogers, Night Of The Hunter, Star In The Dust, Spring Reunion* and many, many others.

The advent of the talkies gave James Gleason the full projection of his personality and the audio appreciation of his thousands of admirers. He had played various characters of the fight game such as fighters, trainers, seconds and managers throughout his career, and when he was placed in the part of the fight manager in *Here Comes Mr. Jordan*, supporting Robert Montgomery, he not only played the part, he produced a living replica of a fight manager, and as such we shall always remember him.

Here Comes Mr. Jordan, (Columbia, 1941).
In this fantasy of the fight game, Robert Montgomery played the part of a fighter with James Gleason playing the part of his fight manager. This picture had a very notable cast which included Claude Rains, Edward Everett Horton, Rita Johnson and Evelyn Keyes. James Gleason's portrayal as the Manager was one of the outstanding performances in the picture and is considered to be one of the best in his whole career.

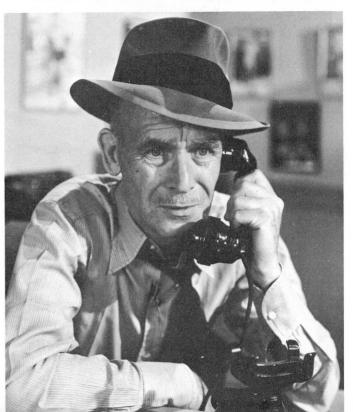

Once Upon A Time,
(Columbia, 1944).
Cary Grant and Janet Blair co-starred in this picture with James Gleason and Ted Donaldson in the supporting roles. This fantasy of the *Dancing Caterpillar* and Cary Grant's attempts to capitalize on the go-go worm created very amusing and original situations. The end of the film came when the caterpillar, through the natural processes of evolution, became a butterfly and flew away.

This Man's Navy, (M.G.M., 1945).
Wally Beery, that famous old screen veteran, along with James Gleason and Tom Drake were costarred in this war picture, and the acting rivalry between Beery and Gleason was a beautiful thing to watch. Luckily, they both won — much to the delight of the viewers.

The Life Of Riley, (Universal, 1949).
William Bendix played the title role in *The Life Of Riley* with James Gleason acting as the perfect foil for his comedy efforts.

DAVID WARK GRIFFITH

Born: January 22, 1874, La Grange, Kentucky. Died: 1948 in Hollywood, California. Height: 6 ft. Weight: 190 lbs. Brown hair, gray eyes.

He was educated at the University of Kentucky. As a boy, Griffith worked in the mail room of his brother's newspaper in a Kentucky town, wrote theatre notes and night police court reports for the Louisville Courier-Journal and witnessed his first theatrical performance, Pete Baker in *America's National Game*. He also saw Julia Marlowe in *Romola* and promptly decided to become a dramatist. He told his ambitions to the manager of the Meffert Stock Company then playing at the Masonic Temple in Louisville. He appeared on the stage for the first time in the role of a dunce in the *District School*. Then came regular periods of stock and road company assignments. He spent several seasons with stock companies and became very successful in many stage plays. He began making moving pictures in Los Angeles in which Mary and Jack Pickford, Henry B. Walthall, and other Biograph players appeared. In 1908 he became assistant director to H. M. Marvin, and Griffith is credited with inventing and developing the flashback, close-up, mist-photography, fade-out and many other revolutionary ideas which caused great gasps of astonishment when first shown on the screen. He was also one of the first directors to make pictures beyond one reel length.

He became internationally famous when he produced and directed *The Birth Of A Nation* and followed it up with the controversial great epic *Intolerance*. His screen credits include: *Hearts Of The World, The Avenging Conscience, Broken Blossoms, The Love Flower, Way Down East, Dream Street, Orphans Of The Storm, One Exciting Night, The White Rose, America, Isn't Life Wonderful, Sally Of The Sawdust*. He went to work for Paramount where he did *The Royal Girl* and *The Sorrows Of Satan*.

DAVID WARK GRIFFITH

He then returned to United Artists after an absence of three years directing *The Drums Of Love* and *Lady Of The Pavements*. *Abraham Lincoln* was his first venture in the talking field; also *The Struggle*. He sold his United Artists partnership in 1933 and until his death, was in retirement.

Rescued From An Eagle's Nest, (Edison, 1907).

This film was written, directed and photographed by Edwin S. Porter, and in this scene of the mountain country we see a young actor by the name of David Wark Griffith as he is about to effect the rescue of a baby who has been abducted and carried away by an eagle to its nest. The action of the abduction was carried out by hidden wires, a stuffed eagle and a live baby who cried lustily throughout all the scenes. D. W. Griffith was to go on to a bigger, greater and a higher destiny.

Intolerance, (D. W. Griffith, 1916). This photo showing the fabulous sets and the thousands upon thousands of people caused a revolution in the film-making of Griffith's era. No one had ever spent so much money, used so many people, built so many sets and covered so many subjects in one film

The Birth Of A Nation, (United Artists, 1915). David Wark Griffith produced one of the greatest pictures of all time and in it he used practically all of the actors and actresses that he had developed with the years. This great cast included Henry B. Walthall, Mae Marsh, Lillian Gish, George Seigman, Spottiswood Aitken, Wallace Reid, Miriam Cooper and many, many others.

Scene at the old Biograph Studio in New York City. We see Robert Herron and Mae Marsh as they await their cue for action from the great master, D. W. Griffith. D. W. Griffith is at the table adjusting a flower vase for the coming scene, and there is little doubt that these painstaking details which this great perfectionist insisted upon throughout his whole career accounted in no small degree for his phenomenal success.

Abraham Lincoln, (United Artists, 1930). Through his boyhood, his early acting career, his stage successes, he had played in many dramas covering various phases of the Great Emancipator. This work and research gained him the knowledge and admiration necessary to produce this picture. His production and direction in this film was a warm, moving portrayal of the life of Abraham Lincoln. He took no liberties with the actual facts, and to all intents and purposes this picture was an actual documentary done with the typical D. W. Griffith overtones, skills and finesses.

ALAN HALE

Born: February 10, 1892, Washington, D. C.
Died: 1950.

Alan Hale's screen career dates back to the days of Biograph and Lubin Studios. His better known parts were in *Covered Wagon, The Four Horsemen* in which he played the Father, and in *Robin Hood* his part was Little John. Among his many, many screen credits were: *The Sap, Sea Ghost,* (1931); in 1934, *Little Man What Now?, Great Expectations, Imitation Of Life, Of Human Bondage, The Lost Patrol, It Happened One Night, The Crusades* (Paramount); in 1937 *The Prince And The Pauper, Stella Dallas, Valley Of The Giants,* and many, many others too numerous to mention.

His career spanned the beginning of the film industry to the transition of the silents into the talkies. He successfully directed many big pictures but his real love and occupation was that of an actor. He was under contract to Warner Bros. for many, many years. His long career and his great lists of screen credits plus his inspired performances in the supporting roles in many of the great spectacular films of our time really have earned him a high place among the screen immortals.

ALAN HALE

An early silent comedy, untitled 1915.

In this comedy he was teamed up with Shirley Mason, one of the top feminine leads of the silent era. In this scene we see Alan Hale at the age of twenty-three in the early stages of his career.

O'Kay, (First National, 1928).

Colleen Moore was the star in this comedy with Alan Hale and Lawrence Gray in the supporting roles. Alan Hale was educated in Philadelphia, Penn. In his early career he was a cub reporter on a Philadelphia newspaper for five years and also wrote stories.

The Adventures Of Marco Polo,
(United Artists, 1938).
Alan Hale supported Gary Cooper in his great starring role as the explorer. This picture was produced with the superb skill and artistry of Samuel Goldwyn.

The Adventures Of Robin Hood
(Warner Bros., 1939).
Costarring Errol Flynn and Olivia De Havilland with Alan Hale playing the part of Little John. Alan Hale had entered pictures in 1914 and he had accomplished what very few actors had before him in the film medium: the ability to work and survive in an ever changing scene. He had watched great stars come and go but his career was constant.

The Adventures Of Don Juan,
(Warner Bros., 1949).

139

JUDY HOLLIDAY

Born; June 21, 1923, New York City. Died: June 7, 1965, New York City.

Height: 5'7". Weight: 130 lbs. Blonde hair and brown eyes.

Her piano teacher-mother left the audience of a Fanny Brice Comedy for New York's Lying-In Hospital just in time for Judy's birth. At four, the youngster was taking ballet lessons, and upon graduation from high school, she studied at Orson Welles' Mercury Theater. Fame came slowly. She played farces on the Eastern Seaboard and more of the same in New York nightclubs.

On Broadway she obtained a role in *Kiss Them For Me* which won her the Clarence Derwent Award of $500.00 for the best supporting actress of the year. For six months after the show closed, Judy looked for a job, and lived with her mother in a furnished room on the award money. Jean Arthur's misfortune proved to be Judy's great break. Illness took Miss Arthur out of the starring role of *Born Yesterday* three days before the play's Philadelphia opening. Stuck with a theater, a play, a cast but no leading lady, the producer, Max Gordon, and playwright Garson Kanin, decided to take a chance on Judy, despite the fact that she was virtually an unknown actress. On a diet of black coffee, she learned the part in three days and opened to rhapsodic notices. A few weeks later, the show premiered in New York to sensational reviews and business. A star was born, and Judy appeared on the stage as Billie Dawn for the next three years.

When Columbia Pictures bought the screen rights to Broadway's most popular comedy, many motion picture actresses were tested for the lead. Eventually Judy was signed to a 7-year contract, and she starred in *Born Yesterday*. Her screen credits include: *Winged Victory, Adam's Rib, Born Yesterday, The Marrying Kind, It Should Happen To You, Phfft, The Solid Gold Cadillac*, and *Bells Are Ringing*.

The true Judy Holliday and "Billie Dawn," the dumb chorine that she played so successfully in *Born Yesterday*, were really two separate and distinct individuals. While Miss Holliday was 5'7" with an I.Q. of 172, she made "Billie Dawn" appear small and stupid. The real girl read Stendhal and Proust. For her sterling performance in *Born Yesterday*, the Academy of Motion Picture Arts and Sciences awarded her the "Oscar" in 1951 as top actress. Her premature death came in 1965.

Adam's Rib, (M.G.M., 1949).
Spencer Tracy and Katharine Hepburn were costarred in this romantic comedy and Judy Holliday, Tom Ewell, David Wayne and Jean Hagen headed the supporting cast. Prior to *Adam's Rib*, she had done small parts in two motion pictures, *Winged Victory* and *Something For The Boys*.

The Solid Gold Cadillac, (Columbia, 1956).
She was costarred with Paul Douglas in this picture. This picture was one of the finest in the closing phases of Paul Douglas' career.

Born Yesterday, (Columbia, 1951).
Judy Holliday had played in *Born Yesterday* when it was a New York Stage success in a theater run of over three years. In this film she was costarred with Broderick Crawford and William Holden, and veteran Director, George Cukor, helped create the picture. This picture brought Judy Holliday the coveted "Oscar" as the best actress for 1951.

It Should Happen To You, (Columbia, 1954).
Judy Holliday, Peter Lawford and Jack Lemmon costarred in this comedy, a satire on the television commercial. In this scene we see the beautiful Judy making a television pitch for a certain brand of soap in a bathtub sequence. Her home was with her mother and child in *The Dakota,* a large old apartment building on Central Park West in New York City.

Bells Are Ringing, (M.G.M., 1960).
The Arthur Freed Production *Bells Are Ringing* had Judy Holliday and Dean Martin rollicking through the song and dance tunes. Vincente Minnelli directed.

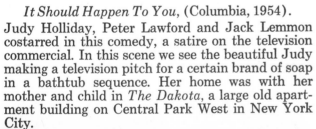

141

JAMES HALL

Born: October 22, 1900, Dallas, Texas. Height: 5'11". Weight: 158 lbs. Light brown hair and brown eyes.

Educated at Dallas, Texas where he was conspicuous as an athlete in baseball, basketball and football. He aspired to theatrical work early in life. When he was twelve years old he used to dance at every amateur night at the Dallas vaudeville house. When he was fourteen years old he ran away with a theatrical company, got as far as Chicago where the show closed. He continued his stage career and when the World War I broke out he enlisted in the first Texas Field Artillery. After the war he continued his stage career and discovered his talents were in musical productions. In the early months of 1926 he was playing the male lead in *Merry Merry* when Jesse Lasky saw him, sensed his screen possibilities and invited him to have a screen test. Two days after the test was made, Hall was placed under a long term contract and sent to Hollywood; the greatest part of his screen career was associated with the Paramount Theaters.

His screen credits include: *The Campus Flirt*; *Hotel Imperial*; *Stranded In Paris*; *Love's Greatest Mistake*, *Ritzy Senorita*; *Rolled Stockings*; *Swim, Girl, Swim*; *Just Married*; *The Fleet's In*; *The Saturday Night Kid*; *Paramount On Parade*; and *Dangerous Dan McGrew*.

He reached the highest point and the greatest role in his career when he was cast opposite Ben Lyon and Jean Harlow in *Hell's Angels*, Howard Hughes' great aviation spectacular.

Smiling Irish Eyes,
(First National Warner Bros., 1929).
James Hall was cast as Rory and Colleen Moore was Kathleen as they endeared themselves to their great following in this rollicking Irish comedy.

The Case Of Lena Smith, (Paramount, 1929).
James Hall was costarred with Emily Fitzroy and Vilma Banky. Miss Fitzroy was one of the greatest character actresses of her era and she was to go on and achieve a great popularity in the horror films. One of Hall's most serious roles was opposite Pola Negri in *Hotel Imperial*.

The Third Alarm, (Tiffany, 1930).
This fire fighting film was a distinct change of pace from the many light leading man roles. From this picture he was to go into *Hell's Angels*, the biggest part of his career.

Hell's Angels, (United Artists, 1930).
This epic was one of the greatest war aviation pictures ever made and created immediate box office stars out of Jean Harlow, James Hall and Ben Lyon. Ben Lyon was in great demand with all the leading ladies in Hollywood and wanted by all the studios.

Millie, (R.K.O., 1931).
In this film James Hall was costarred with Helen Twelvetrees. A roster of Hall's leading ladies read like a "Who's Who In Hollywood." They include Bebe Daniels, Pola Negri, Betty Compson, Clara Bow, Ruth Taylor and Vilma Banky and many others.

OLIVER HARDY

Born: January 18, 1892, Atlanta, Georgia. Height: 6'1". Weight: 284 lbs. Black hair and brown eyes.

He started his stage career in stock four years and he toured the South with his own singing act. His early career in motion pictures was at the old Vitagraph Studios in Hollywood in the years of 1918-25. His last work before going to Hal Roach was with Buck Jones in Fox Features. He was placed under long term contract with Hal Roach and costarred in the Laurel and Hardy comedies.

His screen credits include: *The Rogue Song, They Go Boom, Men Of War, Night Owls, Pack Up Your Troubles,* (M.G.M.) and many, many Laurel and Hardy Comedies.

OLIVER HARDY

Babes In Toyland, (M.G.M., 1934).
For this picture Charlotte Henry was loaned from Paramount and Felix Knight played a supporting role. In this filmed fable of the famous babies in the nursery rhymes, Laurel and Hardy were in their element.

Unaccustomed As We Are,
(M.G.M.—Hal Roach All Talking Comedy).
Laurel and Hardy became as well known on the American scene as ham and eggs. In this scene we see Thelma Todd, Edgar Kennedy, and Laurel and Hardy as they build up a gag to place poor old Stan Laurel in some hopeless predicament.

Bonnie Scotland, (M.G.M., 1935).
Their many years of close association and working together had established a rapport between these two renowned comedians, and as a result, their work was a pure inspiration with instinctive reflex action which insured the success of many a gag and situation. In this picture Laurel and Hardy romped through the crags of old Scotland and set back the old Scottish traditions at least fifty years.

The Flying Deuces, (R.K.O. Radio, Boris Morros Prod., 1939).
This scene from the picture shows Laurel and Hardy fastened securely by ropes to a very large iron weight. The writers of these comedies were forced to be very nimble-witted both in creating a situation like this one and extricating their victims scot free in order to be able to continue with the next gag and situation. Needless to say, both comedians were kept in tip-top physical shape probably from getting into and then trying to get out of the writers' swamps and quagmires.

Night Owls,
(M.G.M.—Hal Roach Comedy).
This immortal team of comedians was always getting into deep water with Stan Laurel providing the "getting" and Oliver Hardy receiving the full benefits and punishments from these situations. This scene shows poor Oliver attempting to negotiate a fence, and Stan Laurel with his usual priceless inspiration, helping Oliver over the fence with disastrous results.

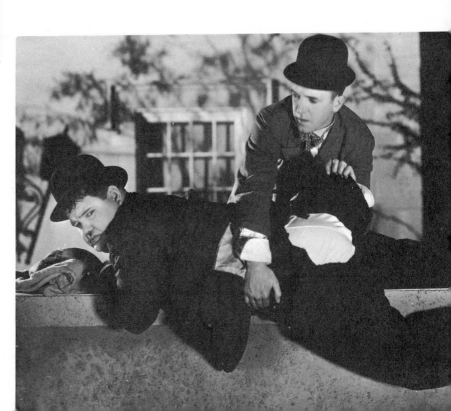

The Return Of Draw Egan, (Ince-Triangle, 1916).
This picture was among the early ones. Louise Glaum, who was one of the great vamps of the silent era, played the feminine lead and Robert McKim played one of his greatest Western heavy roles. William S. Hart's Western costume was an unforgettable trademark—a flat brimmed stetson with four dents, boots rising above the knee and a flowing neckerchief—and most of all a strong, silent expression that expressed a man of granite will.

WILLIAM S. HART

Born: 1870, Newburgh, New York. Died: 1946 in Saugus, California.

Height: 6′1″. Weight: 180 lbs.

He had a distinguished New York stage career starting with his debut at the age of nineteen with Daniel B. Banmann. Upon his arrival in Hollywood, he went to work for Ince. Under his own banner, Hart-Artcraft, he played in *Wolves Of The Trail, Blue Blazes Rawden*. He organized his own company in September, 1919 and did many of his famous Western roles. In 1920 he signed up with Famous Players and starred in *Sand, The Toll Gate*, and *Tumbleweeds*. He also made many fine films of the old West under the Triangle Banner. His pictures were great box-office because his stage training gave him a great acting skill and talent far above the ordinary cowboy hero.

Riddle Gawne, (Artcraft Productions, 1918).
Lon Chaney had just started his career and was playing heavies and villains. Catherine McDonald, at the height of her career, played the feminine lead in this western film, although most of her pictures were of society variety.

Shark Monroe,
(Artcraft Productions, 1918).
William S. Hart again was costarred with Catherine McDonald in this action story of the great Northwest. Hart's rise in Westerns paralleled his devout interest in the West. He owned an amazing collection of Western Art and trappings which can now be seen in Newhall, California high on a hill, at the famous William S. Hart Estate. This shrine holds all his collection and his costumes.

Tumbleweeds, (Paramount, 1925).
In this action scene we see William S. Hart in his usual conflict with one of the heavies. Barbara Bedford, and to the extreme left, Lucien Littlefield, supply the comedy relief. William S. Hart had a selection of old Western guns. In one room of his house he kept the antique revolvers and in another room were the frontier-type rifles.

With Maurice Chevalier in Newall—
1931.
Maurice Chevalier had come over to the United States under contract to Paramount.

ELISSA LANDI

ELISSA LANDI

Born: December 6, 1904. Died: 1948. Height: 5'5". Weight: 120 lbs. Light auburn hair and green eyes. Birthplace: Venice, Italy.

Her stage career led to her London Debut of *The Storm* which ran for five months in England. It was a great success and she followed it with leads in *Lavender Ladies, The Constant Nymph* and many other stage roles. Foreign picture companies immediately snatched her up and she did eight pictures during the next two years. She went to New York to play the role of Catherine Barclay in the stage version of *A Farewell To Arms*. Although the play made no great impression, she did, receiving six motion picture offers. Her first Hollywood part was in *Body And Soul* opposite Charles Farrell.

Her screen credits include: *The Yellow Ticket, Wicked, A Passport To Hell, The Woman In Room Thirteen, The Devil's Lottery, Always Good-bye,* C. B. De Mille's *Sign Of The Cross, The Warrior's Husband, The Masquerader, By Candle Light, I Loved You Wednesday, Man Of Two Worlds* and many others. In addition to her great stage and screen career, Elissa Landi was a successful poet and writer.

The Sign Of The Cross, (Paramount, 1932).

This picture was one of Cecil B. De Mille's fine biblical spectaculars. Elissa Landi was co-starred with Fredric March, Claudette Colbert and Charles Laughton.

148

The Warrior's Husband, (Fox, 1933).
This scene shows Elissa Landi, Ernest Truex and Marjorie Rambeau as they carry on their machinations and intrigues in this film story of old Rome.

Count Of Monte Cristo, (United Artists, 1934).
Elissa Landi costarred with Robert Donat in the film version of the Alexander Dumas Classic.

Enter Madame, (Paramount, 1935).
Directed by Elliott Nugent, Elissa Landi was costarred with Cary Grant, the greatest leading man of the era.

The Great Flirtation, (Paramount, 1934).
Under contract to Paramount she was to make many fine pictures. In this film she shared the starring honors with Adolphe Menjou, David Manners, Raymond Walburn and Lynn Overman. This picture was directed by Ralph Murray.

LESLIE HOWARD

LESLIE HOWARD

Born: April 24, 1893, London, England. Died: 1943. Height: 5'10½". Weight: 145 lbs. Blond hair and blue eyes.

He was educated at Dulwich College in England. His stage experience included *Peg O' My Heart*, *Charley's Aunt*, *The Green Hat*, *The Animal Kingdom* and others. His screen credits include: *Outward Bound*, *A Free Soul*, *Reserved For Ladies*, *The Animal Kingdom*, *Secrets*, *Berkeley Square*, *Captured*, *British Agent*, *The Lady Is Willing*, *Of Human Bondage*, *The Scarlet Pimpernel*. In 1936 he did the film version of *The Petrified Forest* (Warner Brothers); *Romeo and Juliet* (M.G.M.); *It's Love I'm After*, *Stand-In*. He co-directed and appeared in *Pygmalion* (Pascal-G.F.D., an English Production).

In 1939 he was associate producer and appeared in *Intermezzo—A Love Story* (United Artists-Selznick); *Gone With The Wind* (Selznick-M.G.M.. He produced and appeared in *The First Of The Few* (General Film-English). In 1943 he was the producer, director and in the cast of *Spitfire* (R.K.O.). This was his last film.

In his screen career, starting from 1930 to 1943—a span of 13 years, he reached the heights of fame costarred with Mary Pickford, Bette Davis, Norma Shearer, Vivien Leigh, Olivia De Havilland, Ingrid Bergman, Wendy Hiller and practically all of the topflight actresses of his time. While travelling in a plane from Lisbon to London during the Second World War in 1943, he was officially reported killed after being attacked by German fighters. His greatest performance is considered to be his interpretation of "Romeo" to Norma Shearer's "Juliet" produced by M.G.M. in 1936.

Romeo and Juliet, (M.G.M., 1936).
M.G.M. constructed the most beautiful, expansive garden and the finest Renaissance balcony. Norma Shearer as "Juliet" and Leslie Howard as "Romeo" gave an inspired performance in the balcony scene. The greatest actors of the era were meticulously selected by Irving Thalberg to head the notable supporting cast which included John Barrymore, Basil Rathbone, Edna May Oliver, C. Aubrey Smith, Ralph Forbes, and Andy Devine. George Cukor directed.

Secrets, (United Artists, 1933).
Mary Pickford played the feminine lead and Leslie Howard costarred with her in this production.

Pygmalion, (M.G.M., 1938).
Leslie Howard co-directed and played the part of "Professor Higgins" in this English version and film adaptation from the play. Wendy Hiller, one of the finer English actresses, played the part of the English waif, "Eliza Doolittle" who was rescued from the perils of the slums and transformed by Leslie Howard into an elegant lady.

Intermezzo, (United Artists—David Selznick, 1939).
Leslie Howard, as a noted concert violinist, was costarred with Ingrid Bergman, who made her American debut in this film, playing the part of a Governess who becomes involved romantically with her employer. Included in the cast were John Halliday, Edna Best, and Cecil Kellaway. Gregory Ratoff directed.

Gone With The Wind, (M.G.M., 1939).
In this immortal film which David O. Selznick left to the world, Leslie Howard played the part of the Scion of an old Southern family. This picture had a tremendous cast headed by Clark Gable, Vivien Leigh, Olivia De Havilland, Thomas Mitchell and many others.

WALTER HUSTON

Born: April 6, 1884, Toronto, Canada. Died: 1950. Height: 6'. Weight: 180 lbs. Brown hair and hazel eyes.

He left home at the age of eighteen to join a traveling road show. In New York City, he obtained a place in the cast of a company playing *Convict's Stripes*. He returned to the stage in 1909 in his own vaudeville act which enjoyed tremendous success and then became a headliner of the Keith and Orpheum Circuits. He returned to the New York stage and his greatest success was as the old man in Eugene O'Neill's *Desire Under The Elms*. About this time Paramount contracted with Huston to appear in two feature-length productions made at their Long Island Studios: *Gentlemen Of The Press* and *The Lady Lies*. On the completion of these films he was sent to Hollywood to play the role of "Trampas" in the all-talking picture *The Virginian*.

His screen credits include: *The Bad Man, Abraham Lincoln, The Criminal Code, The Star Witness, A Woman From Monte Carlo, A House Divided* and *Law And Order* at Universal. Signed with M.G.M. in 1932 he did *The Beast Of The City, The Wet Parade, American Madness*. For Columbia, *Rain*. For U.A.: *Night Court, Congo, Hell Below, Gabriel Over The White House, The Prize Fighter And The Lady, Dodsworth*. U.A. in 1936: *The Outlaw*.

His genius showed in the title role of Abraham Lincoln and also in scenes with Ruth Chatterton in *Dodsworth*.

WALTER HUSTON

Abraham Lincoln, (United Artists, 1930).
This picture was one of the great highlights of Walter Huston's screen career.

Law And Order, (Universal, 1932).
He starred in this Western with some of the greatest,
Raymond Hatton, Andy Devine and Harry Carey.

Dodsworth, (United Artists, 1936).
This film is listed as one of the greatest hits Samuel
Goldwyn ever produced. The casting of Ruth Chatterton, a great stage personality with Walter Huston created magic chemistry.

The Outlaw, (United Artists, 1943).
Walter Huston was costarred with Jane Russell,
Thomas Mitchell and Jack Buetel.

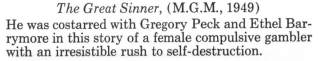

The Great Sinner, (M.G.M., 1949)
He was costarred with Gregory Peck and Ethel Barrymore in this story of a female compulsive gambler
with an irresistible rush to self-destruction.

AL JOLSON

Born: May 28, 1888, St. Petersburg, Russia. Died: 1950. Height: 5'8": Black hair and brown eyes.

He was brought to America as a baby and was picked by his father as the one to follow in his foot-steps and become the sixth in a succession of Jewish Cantors in their family. Against this the boy eventually rebelled and while yet very young he joined the traveling circus as a ballyhoo man, later changing to a cafe entertainer. Family objections were finally overruled and Jolson with his brother and a third man formed a vaudeville act and went on the road for several years. During this time he discovered his peculiar ability to please an audience by confidential chatter and songs from informal places such as the top of the orchestra's piano. A little later, he was advised by an old colored man who was helping him dress, to black his face and see if it did not improve his ability to make an audience laugh. Thus was born the greatest of all black-face comedians and "Mammy" singers. He joined Dockstader's Minstrels and after two years with them he was placed under contract by the Shuberts.

Jolson's climb to stardom on stage and screen was meteoric from that time on. For five years he did the Winter Garden Shows as their great headliner. The silent screen had made fabulous offers but Jolson could not be weaned away from the stage. Then came Vitaphone Pictures and the opportunity to be heard as well as seen from the screen. Jolson consented to try one picture for Warner Bros.

They called it *The Jazz Singer* and it made motion picture history. It was the first full length talking picture ever made and it revolutionized the entire industry. Jolson followed this with *The Singing Fool*, a picture which broke attendance records in all parts of the world.

His film credits include: *Say It With Songs, Big Boy, Mammy* and *Wonder Bar*.

The Jazz Singer, (Warner Bros., 1927).

The Jazz Singer was the first full length talkie picture ever made—a picture that broke box office records, changed entertainment values and revolutionized the entire motion picture industry.

Say It With Songs, (Warner Bros., 1929).
In this picture he costarred with a small boy named Davey Lee. The plot of the story called for a death scene with Davey Lee with Jolson at the bedside.

The Singing Fool, (Warner Bros Production, 1928).

Mammy, (Warner Bros., 1930).
This scene shows Al Jolson with two veterans of the screen, Hobart Bosworth and Lowell Sherman as they lead the parade in a small southern town. He followed this picture with *Big Boy* in the same year and *Wonder Bar* in 1934. In 1939 he did *Rose of Washington Square* and *Swanee River* for Twentieth Century Fox.

Go Into Your Dance,
(Warner Bros., 1935).
In this film he was teamed with Ruby Keeler and Glenda Farrell.

BUCK JONES

Born: December 4, 1889, Vincennes, Indiana. Height: 6′. Weight: 178 lbs. Brown hair and dark blue eyes.

When one year old, he was taken to his Father's 3,000 acre ranch in Red Rock, Oklahoma where he spent his entire boyhood. He began to ride a horse as soon as he could walk, and in his youth he became one of the regular ranch cowboys. Then he joined the United States Army, and served on the Mexican Border. While on general duty with the Army in the Philippines, he was wounded in the thigh by a native's bullet and was finally invalided home to the United States where he received his discharge for disability. In 1914 he became a featured bronco rider and trick roper with the 101 ranch wild west show, and was later featured in the same capacity with the Ringling Brothers-Barnum & Bailey Circus.

In 1917, he entered motion pictures as an extra. Later he did small parts and doubled for Tom Mix, William S. Hart, William Farnum and other stars. Buck Jones' ability as both rider and actor brought him swift advancement, and he quickly became recognized as one of the screen's leading cowboy stars. He developed a tremendous following, especially by the boys of the nation. In his career he starred in more than 200 pictures. His film credits include: *Riders Of The Purple Sage, One Man Trail, Hell's Hole, The Desert Outlaw, The Trail Rider, Durand Of The Bad Lands, The Desert's Price, The Desert Valley, Hills Of Peril, South Of The Rio Grande, The Forbidden Trail, Gordon Of Ghost City*, Universal Serials, and many, many more.

His popularity was evidenced by the fact that "Buck Jones Rangers," a fan organization formed in his honor, had a membership of over two million. In addition, his pictures had a huge outlet abroad, especially in the orient.

Buck Jones And Silver, (Circa, 1930).

Untitled Western, (Fox, Circa 1918)

In this scene we see Marion Nixon playing the feminine lead to Buck Jones. He began his career at the William Fox Studios at $100 a week — a figure that later grew to $2,500 a week. After leaving Fox Studios, he was given a three-year contract by Harry Cohn at Columbia. But he was to do some of his greatest pictures at Universal.

Texas Ranger, (Columbia, 1931).

This scene shows Buck Jones playing the title role of the "Texas Ranger" with Harry Woods in the role of a heavy and Carmelita Geraghty playing the feminine lead. Before he was a motion picture star he was a test driver for racing cars.

West Of The Great Divide, (Monogram).

This film was made in the latter phases of Buck Jones' career. In this scene we see Buck with that great veteran character actor, Raymond Hatton.

Unmarried, (Paramount, 1939).

Buck Jones frequently worked in pictures that were not westerns. He costarred here with Helen Twelvetrees, Donald O'Connor, John Hartley, Dorothy Howe, and Larry Crabbe.

CAROLE LOMBARD

Born: October 6, 1909, Fort Wayne, Indiana. Died: 1942. Height, 5' 2". Weight: 112 lbs. Golden hair and blue eyes.

Carole Lombard started in the Mack Sennett comedy ranks, rose to bits, became a leading woman and then blossomed into stardom.

When she was seven years old, her family arrived in Hollywood. They liked the film capital and became permanent residents. In her school career, there was no indication that Carole Lombard was headed for the screen. It was not until she took a three-year course in a dramatic school that she became ambitious for a film career.

When she went into Mack Sennett comedies, however, she had no thought of eventual stardom. She thoroughly enjoyed the custard pie throwing, the falls into pools, beds of cactus, etc., etc. Her first starring role was for Fox in *Me, Gangster*, (1928) following which she went to work at Pathé and graduated into feminine leads.

She arrived at stardom costarring with Robert Armstrong in *Big News* and *The Racketeer*. Carole Lombard was noted for her lack of temperament and her great acting ability. This combination made her a favorite among directors and placed her in great demand. Her picture credits include: *Man of the World, Ladies' Man, Twentieth Century, We're Not Dressing, Hands Across The Table, My Man Godfrey, Love Before Breakfast, Nothing Sacred, No Man Of Her Own, The Match King,* and others.

In *Twentieth Century*, a Columbia Production, she was costarred with John Barrymore. This film was a theatrical story of a zany producer who, in the course of a transcontinental journey aboard a train, attempts by any means, fair or foul, to coerce, intimidate and woo a temperamental actress to play in his productions. Carole Lombard was in her element of great comedy and gave her most inspired performance.

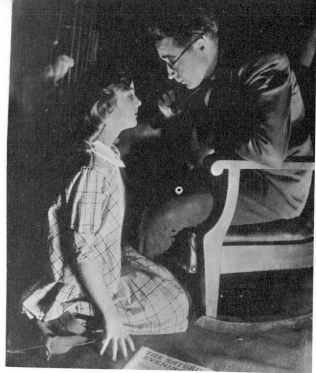

The Perfect Crime, (Paramount, 1921).
Monte Blue was at the height of his film career, and Carole Lombard at the age of 12 played a supporting role in this film with him. As she grew a little bit older, a little more mature, she joined the ranks of many others and became a student in the great Mack Sennett school from which she was to graduate with the highest of comedy honors.

20th Century, (Columbia, 1934).
In this rollicking comedy John Barrymore was costarred with Carole Lombard, with Ralph Forbes, Walter Connolly and Roscoe Karns in the supporting roles. This scene shows the many comedy situations in which John Barrymore and Carole Lombard excelled.

My Man Godfrey, (Universal, 1936).
William Powell, Carole Lombard, Gail Patrick and Alice Brady combined their talents and made a great box-office success out of this comedy epic. William Powell, fresh from his great triumphs at M.G.M., and Carole Lombard, direct from her comedies at Paramount, were superlative.

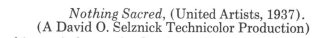

Nothing Sacred, (United Artists, 1937).
(A David O. Selznick Technicolor Production)
In this marital comedy Carole Lombard and Fredric March starred. In this scene, after a hand-to-hand battle the length and breadth of a hotel suite, Carole Lombard is about to lose to Fredric March by a knockout.

To Be Or Not To Be,
(United Artists, 1942).
Carole Lombard and Jack Benny were starred in this European political satire with cloak and dagger overtones. This film was Carole Lombard's last picture, before her untimely, tragic death.

GUY KIBBEE

Born: March 6, 1886, El Paso, Tex.
Died: 1956.

Guy Kibbee was the veteran of over three hundred stage plays. He appeared in *The Torch Song* on the New York Broadway Stage and became immediately famous. His first picture was *Man Of The World* with William Powell, in 1931.

His screen credits include: *Forty-Second Street, Lilly Turner, The Life Of Jimmy Dolan, Gold Diggers Of 1933, Footlight Parade, Lady For A Day, Easy To Love, Havana Widows, Convention City, Wonder Bar, Captain Blood.* His most recent pictures were: *Power Of The Press, Girl Crazy, Romance Of Rosy Ridge* and *Fort Apache.*

His portrayals of grandfathers, old uncles and country cousins convulsed the nation for many years.

GUY KIBBEE

Convention City, (First National and Vitaphone Picture, Warner Bros. 1933).

In this political comedy Joan Blondell played the feminine lead. His contemporaries and intimate friends in Hollywood were Pat O'Brien, Frank McHugh, James Cagney and Walter Catlett. Kibbee was reputed to have a new story to tell every time he met them.

Don't Bet On Blondes, (Warner Bros., 1935).

In this film Guy Kibbee played the part of Colonel Youngblood, an old Southern Colonel. The beautiful Claire Dodd played one of the blondes.

160

Captain Blood, (Warner Bros., 1935).
In this great spectacular of Rafael Sabatini's Pirate Sea Story, Errol Flynn was to launch his meteoric career. In the great cast supporting him were the actors in this scene: Robert Barratt, Guy Kibbee. Ross Alexander and J. Carroll Naish.

Captain January, (Fox, 1936).
Shirley Temple and Guy Kibbee headed a superb cast which included June Lang, Buddy Ebsen, Slim Summerville and Jane Darwell.

Three Comrades, (M.G.M., 1938).
Franchot Tone and Robert Young, with Robert Taylor were the Three Comrades. Margaret Sullivan played the feminine lead, and Guy Kibbee portrayed Alfonse the Bartender.

PERCY KILBRIDE

Born: July 16, 1888 in San Francisco, California. He began his stage career in road and stock companies and then graduated to Broadway in *Those We Love* and *George Washington Slept Here*. He had done over eight hundred roles in his stage career and he made his motion picture debut in 1942.

His screen credits include: *Black Bart, You've Got To Stay Happy, You Were Meant For Me, Soft Touch, Sun Comes Up, Free For All* and he gained his bid to posterity in the *Ma And Pa Kettle* series for Universal.

PERCY KILBRIDE

Ma And Pa Kettle, (Universal, 1949).
Marjorie Main played Ma and Percy Kilbride played Pa. In this action scene we see them having a short altercation which Ma won, as usual.

Ma And Pa Kettle Go To Town, (Universal-International, 1950).
Percy Kilbride and Marjorie Main were supported by Meg Randall and Dick Long.

Ma And Pa Kettle At The Fair,
(Universal-International, 1952).
In this scene Ma and Pa Kettle hit upon
an idea for getting enough money together
to send Rosie Kettle to college. The part of
Rosie Kettle was played by Lori Nelson.

Ma And Pa Kettle On Vacation, (Universal, 1953).
In the latter part of his career Percy Kilbride was hit by an
automobile and never fully recovered from this accident which
finally led to his death.

Ma And Pa Kettle At Home,
(Universal-International, 1954).
This scene shows Pa and Ma Kettle with
their spruced-up brood, as they proudly
await the coming of the Farm Improve-
ment Inspector.

VICTOR McLAGLEN

Born: December 11, 1886, Tunbridge Wells, Kent, England. Died: 1959. Height: 6'3". Weight 220 lbs. Dark brown hair and deep blue eyes.

When Victor was a little boy the family moved to North West London and it was there that he attended St. Boniface School for Boys from which he graduated at the age of fourteen. After six weeks in the quiet surroundings of Tunbridge Wells, Victor began to long for travel. With the consent of his parents he sailed for Canada. After several years there he traveled the entire world and finally in the year of 1914 he traveled in Africa with a family vaudeville act but the World War was coming on, and they took a boat immediately out of Cape Town to England. Victor McLaglen became a Lieutenant and went through World War I with a very distinguished record, being cited for bravery. At the end of the War he had been promoted to Captain. One evening at the National Sporting Club in London, Mr. I. B. Davidson, one of the important film directors in England, signed him up for *The Call Of The Road*. Following this success, McLaglen played in British pictures for four years. J. Stuart Blackton signed McLaglen for the leading male role in *The Glorious Adventure*. In 1924, J. Stuart Blackton cabled McLaglen to come to Hollywood, all travel expenses paid to play the leading role in *The Beloved Brute*. McLaglen's work in the picture *Wings Of Chance* won him a long term contract with First National.

Fox Film had begun casting for the new film *What Price Glory*, Directed by Raoul Walsh. McLaglen was engaged for the role of Captain Flagg and before the picture was finished Winfield Sheehan, in charge of production, arranged to buy McLaglen's contract from First National. Fox Film signed him for a five year term and it was renewed several times. McLaglen made many outstanding pictures including the *Black Watch*, directed by John Ford, who also directed *The Informer; The Cock-Eyed World* still holds the record for the World's Box Office Attendance at the Roxy Theater in New York, during the week McLaglen appeared there in person. $170,000 was taken in.

Upon his return to Hollywood he was engaged by R.K.O. to appear in *The Informer*. His picture credits include: *The Fighting Heart, Beau Geste, A Devil With Women, Women Of All Nations, The Informer, Under Two Flags, Wee Willie Winkie, Rackety Rax, The Lost Patrol, Professional Soldier*, etc. His starring role as *The Informer* places him forever as one of our greatest screen immortals.

What Price Glory, (Fox, 1926). Directed by Raoul Walsh. This picture was the turning point of his career. His many years of Army Service enabled him to live the part of a Soldier. He was teamed up with Edmund Lowe and Dolores Del Rio.

164

Women Of All Nations, (Fox, 1931).
Victor McLaglen who played the part of Captain Flagg and Edmund Lowe as Sergeant Quirt teamed up again in this picture and once more they smashed box office records all over the country.

Cock-Eyed World, (Fox, 1929).
Directed by Raoul Walsh this picture was McLaglen's second talking picture and again he costarred with Edmund Lowe. When McLaglen's contract with Fox Film expired, he free-lanced for several months and then toured the country in a vaudeville sketch with Edmund Lowe, who played Sergeant Quirt in *What Price Glory* and *The Cock-Eyed World.*

The Informer, (R.K.O., 1935).
Victor McLaglen reached the heights of his great acting career when he starred in the title role. This story of the Irish Rebellion gave McLaglen full scope of all his talent and life long experience and of all the memorable pictures in which he worked *The Informer* was his masterpiece.

Wee Willie Winkie, (Twentieth Century Fox, 1937).
Shirley Temple, the greatest child attraction of the motion pictures, was costarred with McLaglen in Rudyard Kipling's immortal classic and their scenes together were both heart warming and poignant.

ALAN LADD

ALAN LADD

Born: September 3, 1913, Hot Springs, Arkansas.

Studied screen acting at the Universal Studios. He was a reporter, advertising manager, and a salesman. He then worked as a grip at Warner Bros. Studios and in "bit" roles until *Rulers Of The Sea*, 1939.

His screen credits include: *And Now Tomorrow, Blue Dahlia, Two Years Before The Mast, Duffy's Tavern, Whispering Smith, Star Spangled Rhythm, Wild Harvest, Beyond Glory, Botany Bay, Desert Legion*. The pictures in the latter part of his career were: *Drum Beat, McConnell Story, Big Land, Boy On A Dolphin, The Deep Six, Proud Rebel, The Bandleaders, Guns In The Timberland, All The Young Men, Orazio, Thirteen West Street* and *The Carpetbaggers*.

His death in his early fifties interrupted the complete fulfillment of his career. But he had left a great heritage of unforgettable roles. *Shane*, in which he played the title role, definitely placed him among the great immortals of the film.

The Right Man or
Her First Romance,
(Monogram Productions,
1940).
In this production Alan Ladd was costarred with Julie Bishop. This film is supposed to be among his very first.

Two Years Before The Mast, (Paramount, 1945).
This story was adapted from the great novel of Richard Henry Dana. Alan Ladd was costarred with Brian Donlevy, William Bendix, and Barry Fitzgerald. This picture was directed by John Farrow.

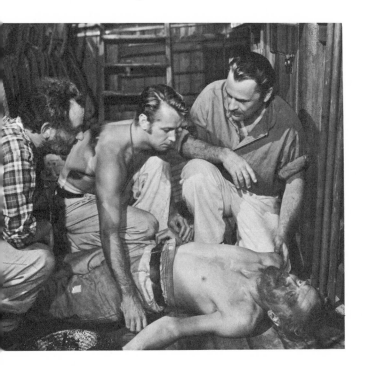

Quantrell's Raiders, (Paramount, 1950).
This picture with its story based on the Confederate Guerrillas costarred Alan Ladd and John Ireland.

Shane, (Paramount, 1951).
Alan Ladd and Jean Arthur were costarred in this film. This role is acknowledged to be Alan Ladd's greatest portrayal. He was voted one of the ten best money-making stars, Motion Picture Herald-Fame Poll for 1947, 1953 and 1954.

Saskatchewan, (Universal, 1954).
Shelley Winters and J. Carroll Naish were costarred with Alan Ladd in this epic of the early days of the Northwest Mounties. In this action scene we see them as they use the Canadian Waterways to escape hostile Indians.

167

JEANETTE MACDONALD

JEANETTE MacDONALD

Born: June 18, 1907, Philadelphia, Pennsylvania. Height 5'5". Weight: 125 lbs. Red-gold hair and blue-green eyes. At 3 years of age she sang a solo at a recital given at a dancing school. The ambition that was born then never relaxed until she achieved stardom. She went to public school and studied dancing, and when she was 7, her sister, Blossom, joined a Broadway Revue.

She visited Blossom at the theatre and met the producer. Jeanette's initial stage appearance was at the Capitol Theater. After several small roles, she came to the attention of Henry W. Savage. He cast her in the leading role as Mitzi in *The Magic Ring*, and Jeanette was on her way to stardom. She gained distinction in the prima donna roles in *Tip Toes; Yes, Yes, Yvette; Sunny Days* and *Angela*.

While she was appearing in *Angela*, she accepted an offer to appear in *The Love Parade*, from Ernst Lubitsch, the great German director in her first screen effort. This production was a great box-office success and established her as a top-flight star. Her screen credits include: *The Vagabond King, Monte Carlo, One Hour With You* and *Love Me Tonight*, all for Paramount; for M.G.M. she did *The Cat And The Fiddle* and *The Merry Widow* in 1934. The costarring of Nelson Eddy and Jeanette MacDonald occurred when they were teamed up in *Naughty Marietta* (1935), which began M.G.M.'s successful series of musicals which included *Rose Marie, Maytime, The Girl Of The Golden West, Sweethearts, New Moon, Bittersweet* and *I Married An Angel*. Another very successful film was *San Francisco* in which she costarred with Clark Gable and Spencer Tracy.

The Love Parade,
(Paramount, 1929).
This picture was made in the momentous year of 1929 when few enterprises could compete against the depression. Even so *The Love Parade* marched on to a box-office triumph. She was costarred with Maurice Chevalier in her screen debut. She also was costarred with Chevalier in *One Hour With You*, (Paramount, 1932) and *Love Me Tonight*, (Paramount, 1933).

The Merry Widow, (M.G.M., 1934).

M.G.M. produced the second version of Franz Lehar's immortal operetta, *The Merry Widow*. The silent version in 1925 costarred John Gilbert and Mae Murray. This 1934 version costarred Jeanette MacDonald and Maurice Chevalier. The supporting cast was headed by Edward Everett Horton, Una Merkel and George Barbier.

Naughty Marietta, (M.G.M., 1935).

This film was an historical motion picture event as it was her first costarring role with Nelson Eddy. The motion picture cycle had just turned, and the musicals were becoming very popular. In *Naughty Marietta* Nelson Eddy's fine baritone voice and Jeanette MacDonald's soprano blended perfectly. She was known as Hollywood's "First Lady of Song."

Smilin' Through, (M.G.M., 1941).

She had married Gene Raymond in 1937, and in the year 1941 M.G.M. revived Norma Shearer's great triumph, *Smilin' Through*, as a vehicle for Jeanette MacDonald, with Gene Raymond playing the part of the discarded lover. Costarring were Brian Aherne and Ian Hunter. Their marriage was not the typical "Hollywood" marriage. Deeply devoted to one another, they carried out the true marriage tradition "Till Death Do Us Part."

San Francisco, (M.G.M., 1936).

Clark Gable, Jeanette MacDonald, Spencer Tracy were costarred with Jack Holt, Ted Healy and Jessie Ralph in the supporting roles. This was a story of old San Francisco dating back to the Barbary Coast and the great earthquake. Clark Gable played the part of a gambling house proprietor, Spencer Tracy played the part of a priest with Jeanette MacDonald singing both popular and operatic airs in this picture. The earthquake sequences were even better than the real quake!

169

MARIO LANZA

MARIO LANZA

Born: January 31, 1921. Died: October 7, 1959. Birthplace: Philadelphia, Pa. Educated in the Berkshire School of Music; performed in Victor Recordings. He was successful on radio and concert tours.

His screen credits include: *That Midnight Kiss, Toast Of New Orleans, The Great Caruso, Because You're Mine* and *Serenade.* He did an appearance in *Winged Victory* and *Seven Hills Of Rome.*

Mario Lanza's short, tempestuous career embraced radio, concert, opera, recording and the motion picture. Lanza was the first vocalist in the history of Victor Red Seal to receive a golden disc (for *Be My Love*). He was the first singer in recording history to sell two and a half million albums. He received the greatest royalty check ever given a singer for a ten month period — $746,000 in 1951.

For the first time in motion picture history, the cameras stayed on the close-up of an artist for the full length of an aria when Lanza sang "Celeste Aida" in *That Midnight Kiss.*

His death at thirty-eight years of age was a shock to all his admirers and followers.

That Midnight Kiss, (M.G.M., 1949).
Mario Lanza the singer and Jose Iturbi, the pianist, were costarred. This picture was Lanza's screen debut.

The Toast Of New Orleans,
(M.G.M., 1950).
In this scene Kathryn Grayson and David Niven seemed embarrassed at Mario Lanza's outburst of song. Lanza could sing D flat over high C with ease. In 1947, he drew 76,000 people in Chicago's Grant Park during two concert appearances. Hollywood sat up and took notice.

The Great Caruso, (M.G.M., 1951).
History repeats itself! Richard Hageman, who conducted the orchestra while Enrico Caruso sang "Vesti La Giubba" from *Pagliacci* in the 1917 Liberty Bond Drive at the Metropolitan Opera House, directed Mario Lanza in the identical scene for this film. Richard Thorpe directed and Joe Pasternak produced. The cast included Ann Blyth and Dorothy Kirsten.

Because You're Mine, (M.G.M., 1952).
Alexander Hall directed and Joe Pasternak produced. The cast included James Whitmore, Doretta Morrow, Paula Corday and Spring Byington. Mario Lanza was unhappy with the story outline of this film and carried out his acting chores in this picture unwillingly.

Seven Hills Of Rome,
(M.G.M., 1958).
This picture was filmed entirely in Italy, costarring Mario Lanza, Marisa Allasio, Renato Rascel and featuring Peggie Castle. It was a heart warming comedy-drama with music, directed by Roy Rowland and produced by Lester Welch.

171

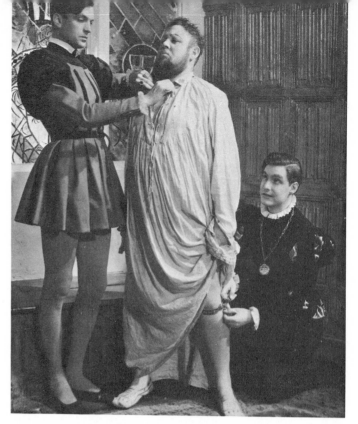

The Private Life Of Henry VIII,
(London Film Production Limited, 1933).
Released through United Artists, this picture is considered to be one of Charles Laughton's greatest characterizations. In this scene John Loder at the left is assisted by Robert Donat, who made his debut in this picture and went on to carve out a brilliant career.

CHARLES LAUGHTON

Born: July 1, 1899, Scarborough, England.
Died: 1962.

His early career started on the London stage and his stage credits were: *The Government Inspector, The Pillars Of Society, The Cherry Orchard, Lilliom, Alibi, Payment Deferred* and others. He was brought from England to play the part "Captain Bligh" in *The Mutiny On The Bounty* starring Clark Gable. The smashing success of this picture gained him immediate star stature.

His screen credits include: *If I Had A Million, White Woman, Sign Of The Cross, Island Of Lost Souls, Les Miserables, Ruggles Of Red Gap, Private Life Of Henry VIII, Barretts Of Wimpole Street, Mutiny On The Bounty* and *Rembrandt.* In 1937 in partnership with Eric Pommer they formed the Mayflower Pictures Corporation and with Laughton as the star they produced *The Beachcomber, Jamaica Inn, Hunchback Of Notre Dame, The Sidewalks Of London, They Knew What They Wanted, It Started With Eve.* His recent pictures include: *Captain Kidd, Paradine Case, The Big Clock, The Bride, Witness For The Prosecution, Spartacus, Under Ten Flags* and *Advise And Consent.*

He shall be forever remembered as the implacable "Captain Bligh" in *The Mutiny On The Bounty.*

Ruggles Of Red Gap, (Paramount, 1935).
In this film Charles Laughton played the English Gentleman costarred with Zasu Pitts, Charlie Ruggles and Lillian Leighton. The story of an English valet amongst some very rich Westerners created some of the most comical situations ever shown on the screen.

Mutiny On The Bounty
(M.G.M., 1935).
Produced by Irving Thalberg and
Directed by Frank Lloyd, costarring
Charles Laughton, Clark Gable and
Franchot Tone.

*The Hunchback of
Notre Dame,* (R.K.O., 1939).

Spartacus,
(Universal-International, 1960).
This scene shows Laurence Olivier,
left, discussing Roman Military pol-
icy with Charles Laughton, right,
and John Gavin. This film also costarred Kirk Douglas, Jean Simmons, Tony Curtis and Peter
Ustinov. *Spartacus* was filmed at the
cost of twelve million dollars.

STAN LAUREL

Born: June 16, 1895, Ulverston, England. Height: 5'10". Weight: 150 lbs. Auburn hair and blue eyes.

He was educated at the King James Grammar School, Bishop Auckland, England. When he was 17 years old, he joined Fred Karno's London comedians as understudy of Charlie Chaplin who was the featured player. Prior to joining up with Karno he received his stage training in a circus, musical comedy, drama and vaudeville. The Karno troupe came to the United States in 1910, where they toured from coast to coast for three and a half years, and then disbanded. Stan Laurel stayed in this country and took a whirl at pictures at Universal in 1917. He then returned to the vaudeville stage, but in 1922 he returned to the screen in Hal Roach comedies. There he met Oliver Hardy, his perfect foil, and his real success began. Together, Laurel and Hardy were to do approximately 40 comedies.

Their screen credits include the aforementioned comedies for Hal Roach. In the latter part of their career, they made a series of Hal Roach comedies under the M.G.M. banner: *The Rogue Song*, 1929; *Babes In Toyland, Bonnie Scotland, The Bohemian Girl, Our Relations, Pick A Star, Swiss Miss, Blockheads, Flying Deuces*. Their concluding films were *Air Raid Wardens, Jitterbugs, The Dancing Masters, Good Neighbors, The Big Noise, The Bullfighters* and many others.

These comedians not only were very successful in their silent comedies but were also very great in their comedy talkies. Both of them had many years of stage training, and as a result had no difficulty when the talking pictures appeared. In fact, the talkies enhanced their comedy routines for now we heard Stan Laurel when he started sniff'ling and broke into tears under Oliver Hardy's abuse.

Your Darn Tootin',
(Hal Roach Comedy, 1928).
No pictorial biography of Stan Laurel would be complete without a scene showing him about to burst into tears. Oliver Hardy gazes at him with his usual baffled exasperation.

A Chump At Oxford,
(Hal Roach, 1940).
In this scene Stan Laurel assumes a naively innocent expression as the Professor, played by Clifford Smith, scolds the repentant Oliver Hardy. It is little known to his fans that Stan Laurel in the very early part of his career both directed and wrote comedies for Hal Roach and at the same time was appearing as a comedian in many of his own creations.

Great Guns, (Fox, 1941).
This film was a military comedy based upon the assumption that Stan and Oliver had been drafted into the United States Army. The beauteous Sheila Ryan played the feminine lead, as Laurel and Hardy proceeded to slow down the United States Army with their comedy routines. This picture is considered to be one of their funniest. They had just been put under contract to 20th Century-Fox.

Jitterbugs,
(20th Century-Fox, 1943).

In this film Stan and Oliver operated a two-man band in a traveling carnival. Their manipulations of these various musical instruments by means of wires, pulleys, and levers is considered to be one of their funniest routines. Another comedy highlight of the picture occurs when they meet a character who has a substitute for gas by placing a tablet in a specified quantity of water. Their gullibility and subsequent developments in trying to sell this revolutionary idea lead to some mirth-provoking routines.

The Dancing Masters,
(20th Century-Fox, 1943).

In this picture they were partners in a ballet dancing school. In the face of a dearth of dancing pupils with eviction staring them in the face, they pitifully attempt to give a lesson to a pupil while the landlord moves out the furniture and equipment.

MARILYN MONROE

Born: June 1, 1926, Los Angeles, Calif.
Died: August 5, 1962, Los Angeles, Calif.
Height: 5′5½″. Weight: 118 lbs. Blonde hair and blue eyes.

She was educated at the Emerson Jr. High School in Los Angeles and the Van Nuys High School in Van Nuys, Calif. Marilyn's real name was Norma Jean Baker. She had a very tragic childhood, in a series of private homes and orphanages. She was eventually taken in by a Mrs. Anna Loower of West Los Angeles, who Marilyn knew as "Aunt Anna." She finally completed her schooling at the Van Nuys High School in the San Fernando Valley and went to work for the Radio Plane Company inspecting parachutes for target planes. After being defeated in several efforts to break into the motion pictures, she finally engaged a room at the Studio Club, home of many an aspiring starlet, and limited herself to two meals a day. One day she was approached by an agent who told her Lester Cowan was producing *Love Happy* and needed a blonde for Groucho Marx to chase. She rushed over and was hired on the spot. The scene lasted for a full minute.

When the picture was released, Cowan persuaded Marilyn to go on tour and plug the picture in Chicago, Detroit, New York and other cities. She did everything — press interviews, TV appearances, charity shows and picked up a lot of poise in the process.

When she returned from the tour, 20th Century-Fox gave her a part in *A Ticket To Tomahawk* in which she played a dancing girl. From there she was requested to read for Director John Huston for a role in *Asphalt Jungle*, in which she played the "niece" of Louis Calhern. The role was a minor one, but when Marilyn came on the screen, the audience gasped. Then 20th Century-Fox picked her for a part in *All About Eve*.

When Darryl Zanuck saw the rushes, he sent for Marilyn's agent and signed her to a long term contract. Her screen credits include: *Scudda Hoo! Scudda Hay!, Let's Make It Legal, Clash By Night, Don't Bother To Knock, We're Not Married, Monkey Business, Gentlemen Prefer Blondes, How To Marry A*

MARILYN MONROE

Millionaire, River Of No Return, There's No Business Like Show Business, The Seven Year Itch, Bus Stop, The Prince And The Showgirl, Some Like It Hot, Let's Make Love, The Misfits, and others.

True, she was a sex symbol. Yet her luscious sex appeal was only part of an extremely remarkable woman. She had already been acclaimed as a comedienne and a musical comedy star, but she was a serious student of the drama with the ambition for strong dramatic roles.

177

Gentlemen Prefer Blondes,
(20th Century-Fox, 1953).
20th Century-Fox resurrected Anita Loos' musical stage play *Gentlemen Prefer Blondes* as a starring vehicle for Marilyn Monroe. Not content with one sex symbol, they also chose Jane Russell, the gorgeous brunette to costar. That grand old veteran, Charles Coburn, played the part of the susceptible millionaire.

The Seven Year Itch, (20th Century-Fox, 1955).
In this scene we see Marilyn standing on an air grate when a sudden rush of air billowed her skirts to the unconcealed delight of the New York pedestrians. This photo of Marilyn was shown in newspapers and magazines and periodicals all over the world. It can be likened to Betty Grable's famous pin-up picture which was sent to the servicemen in the Second World War.

The River of No Return,
(20th Century-Fox, 1954).
Marilyn Monroe was costarred with Robert Mitchum and Rory Calhoun. This picture was, in the main, a serious drama.

Some Like It Hot,
(United Artists, 1959).
Marilyn Monroe was costarred with Jack Lemmon and Tony Curtis in this delightful comedy. Lemmon and Curtis, through financial straits, are forced to don women's clothes and join a girls' band. Billy Wilder directed this picture. Pat O'Brien, George Raft and Joe E. Brown were in the supporting roles.

The Misfits, (United Artists, 1961). Clark Gable and Marilyn Monroe were costarred in this picture. In the supporting cast were Montgomery Clift and Thelma Ritter. One of the greatest directors of our time, John Huston, directed this story. The filming was done in the summer in Nevada with temperatures in the hundreds. The violent scenes and physical exertion in this kind of weather undoubtedly contributed to Clark Gable's death. Ironically, this picture was also to be Marilyn Monroe's last.

ADOLPHE MENJOU

Born: February 18, 1890, Pittsburgh, Penna. Died: Los Angeles, California. Height: 5'10". Weight: 153 lbs. Dark brown hair and dark blue eyes.

His father, Albert Menjou, a hotel proprietor of considerable means, saw to it that his son received a good education at Culver Military Academy and at Cornell University. The youth studied mechanical engineering but devoted a good deal of his time to writing, producing, directing and acting in plays for the Cornell Theatrical group. After completing his education, he joined the McLaughlin stock company in Cleveland, Ohio in 1912. Later that year, he did his first motion picture work—with the old Vitagraph Company in New York City. He was cast as a suave man of the world, and he made screen love to such stars as Marguerite Clark and Norma Talmadge.

When World War I broke out, he immediately enlisted, saw service in Italy and France and by the time of his discharge, had risen to the rank of Captain. After the war, he moved to California with the growing motion picture business. His most notable success in a leading role was in *A Woman Of Paris* in which he costarred with Edna Purviance. This film was unique in the fact that it was written and directed by Charlie Chaplin and was the only picture in which he himself did not appear. When sound came to the screen, Menjou was well equipped, because of his stage training, to continue in the fore-front of character actors. During his long career, he did over 220 films.

His screen credits include: *The Sheik, The Three Musketeers, A Woman Of Paris, The Grand Duchess And The Waiter, The Front Page, Morning Glory, A Farewell To Arms, The Trumpet Blows,* (Paramount) and others.

For many years Menjou had been recognized as one of the best-dressed men in the world, and his name constantly appeared on "Best Dressed" lists compiled by fashion experts from all parts of the globe. His autobiography was titled, appropriately enough, *It Took Nine Tailors.*

ADOLPHE MENJOU

The World's Applause, (Paramount, 1923). (A William De Mille Production).
Bebe Daniels, Lewis Stone, Kathlyn Williams, Harrison Ford and Adolphe Menjou played the leads in this Paramount silent production. Kathlyn Williams, in the early days of the silents, had been one of the greatest serial queens of the American Screen. William De Mille was one of the great directors in the early days of Paramount, and was a brother to the famous Cecil B. De Mille.

A Woman Of Paris, (United Artists, 1923).
Charles Chaplin produced and directed this picture because of his complete faith in the superior acting abilities of his leading woman in many comedies, Edna Purviance. Adolphe Menjou costarred with her, and between them, they created a superior picture with credit due to Charles Chaplin's writing the story and directing the picture.

This Tiger Lady, (Paramount, 1928).
Evelyn Brent and Adolphe Menjou costarred in this film. In this scene we see them together, and to bear out the title, even the tiger!

Sing, Baby, Sing, (20th Century-Fox, 1936).
Alice Faye, Gregory Ratoff, Ted Healy, Patsy Kelly, Michael Whalen, The Ritz Brothers, and Adolphe Menjou created a sterling musical-comedy. This picture gave Menjou a chance to demonstrate his comedy talents, and he acquitted himself very well among this great group of leading comedians of the era. In *The Front Page*, (United Artists), one of the finest newspaper films ever made, Adolphe Menjou played one of his greatest parts as the garrulous managing editor.

One Hundred Men and A Girl, (Universal, 1937).
This picture was one of the Deanna Durbin musical films. The great conductor, Leopold Stokowski, is shown in this scene, trapped between two aspiring musicians, Mischa Auer and Adolphe Menjou.

181

TOM MIX

TOM MIX

Born: January 6, 1880, near Mix Run, Pa.
Died: 1940. Height: 6'. Weight: 165 lbs.
Black hair and brown eyes.

His stage experience was gathered in
vaudeville in 1928. He was a member of
the rough riders during the Spanish-
American War. He also was a United
States Deputy Marshal in Oklahoma.
When he was a trick rider in the Rodeos
he attracted attention of a movie director
and was quickly signed to play in the movies. He became one of the biggest stars on
the Fox Lot. At the top of his fame he
received as much as $20,000 a week.

His screen credits include: *The Drifter,
King Cowboy, The Dude Ranch, Out-
lawed, Flaming Guns, The Fourth Horse-
man, Hidden Gold, My Pal The King,
The Terror Trail, Rustlers Round-Up* and
Destry Rides Again, etc.

He is recorded in motion picture history
as one of our greatest Western Actors. He
was the hero image of all the children in
the United States at that time. His films
were scrupulous works of high morality.

Coming Of The Law,
(Fox, 1918).
The cast in this picture from
right to left was: Tom Mix,
Jane Novak, George Nichols
and Charles Le Moyne. Tom
Mix was a Texas Ranger in his
youth, discovered by the great
producer William M. Selig and
starred in Selig's version of
Zane Grey's western novel,
The Thundering Herd.

Stunt Scene Tom Mix, (Universal).

Tom Mix and Tony were game for anything. In this stunt scene Tony is carrying Tom and a dummy over an iron gate. Tom Mix rode "Tony" his famous mount in at least eight pictures a year for over a dozen years, performing some of the most hazardous rides, jumps and stunts that the screen has ever known.

Painted Post, (Fox, 1928).

Because Tom Mix would never allow a double to take risks greater than himself, he suffered injuries but, in each case, recovered very quickly.

Destry Rides Again, (Universal, 1932).

This tense action scene shows Tom Mix in a typical gun fight in a Western saloon. His opponent facing him was Francis Ford, a great western star in his own right and the brother of John Ford, one of the screen's finest directors.

The Fourth Horseman, (Universal, 1933).

Tom Mix was noted for his fight and action scenes with the bad men and villains of the screen. In this action scene we see Tom Mix rescuing Margaret Lindsay from the clutches of Fred Kohler who turned out to be one of the screen's greatest "badmen."

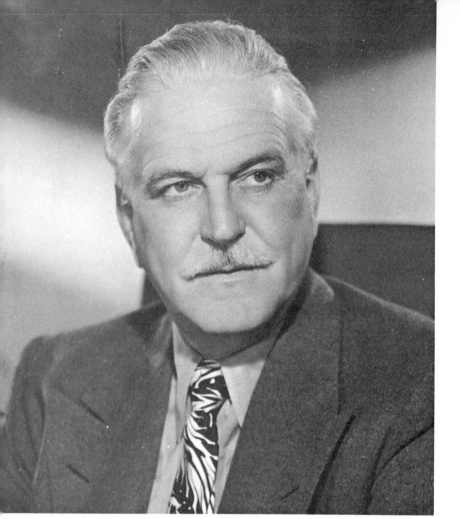

FRANK MORGAN

Born: June 1, 1890. New York City, New York. Died: 1949. Height: 6'. Weight: 180 lbs. Light brown hair and gray with brown eyes.

He was educated in public and private schools and Cornell University. He was born of a wealthy family in New York City. In his youth he played in vaudeville and then naturally gravitated to the New York Stage. Among his stage credits are: *Mr. Wu, Rosalie, The Man Who Came Back, Seventh Heaven, Gentlemen Prefer Blondes, Topaz, Firebrand* and *Rockabye*.

His screen credits are too numerous and varied to be mentioned here. Accordingly, the following are his most successful pictures under his contract at M.G.M. Studios: *Reunion In Vienna, When Ladies Meet, Broadway To Hollywood, Naughty Marietta, The Great Ziegfeld, Saratoga, Rosalie, Sweethearts, The Wizard Of Oz, The Mortal Storm, Boom Town, The Vanishing Virginian, Tortilla Flat* with Spencer Tracy, Hedy Lamarr and John Garfield, *Human Comedy* with Mickey Rooney. With the completion of *Any Number Can Play* in 1949 costarring Clark Gable, Morgan's career ended.

His death came at the age of 59. In *The Wizard Of Oz*, as the "Wizard," Frank Morgan was outstanding.

FRANK MORGAN

The Perfect Gentleman, (M.G.M., 1936).

Frank Morgan was costarred with Cicely Courtneidge, a top rank English star who was making her American Film debut. Frank Morgan played a scapegrace, lovable, down-at-heel, old Army Major who hitches his wagon to a music hall star. The supporting cast included: Heather Angel, Richard Waring, Forrester Harvey and Una O'Connor.

Courage Of Lassie, (M.G.M., 1946).
The Lassie dog pictures proved to be a box-office bonanza to the M.G.M. studios and also a training school for aspiring actors and actresses. In this scene we see a young girl, Elizabeth Taylor, in conversation with Frank Morgan. For practically a decade Elizabeth Taylor, from girlhood to womanhood, appeared in films with all the topflight stars at M.G.M. Undoubtedly, Frank Morgan contributed his part to teaching this young tyro the tried and true methods of the stage and screen.

Summer Holiday, (M.G.M., 1948).
Summer Holiday was a musical remake of *Ah, Wilderness,* Eugene O'Neill's play. Costarred in the cast were Walter Huston, Mickey Rooney, Agnes Moorehead, Frank Morgan and many others. In the 17 years that he worked for M.G.M. he made 68 film roles. *Key To The City* was to be the last role he would play.

Dimples, (Fox, 1936).
At the tender age of six years Shirley Temple played the title role of "Dimples" for Fox Studios. Frank Morgan was loaned out by M.G.M. to play the part of her guardian. Helen Westley, one of our finest actresses, and Stepin Fetchit were in the supporting cast.

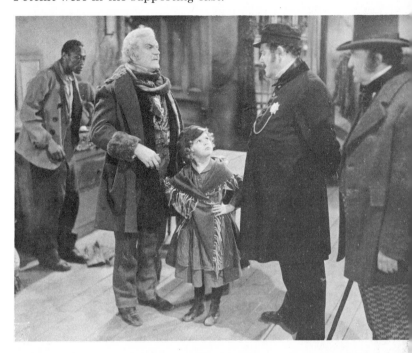

Any Number Can Play, (M.G.M., 1949).
This picture preceded his last one. In it he costarred with Clark Gable and Alexis Smith.

BELA LUGOSI

BELA LUGOSI

Born: October 20, 1884, Lugos, Hungary. Died: 1956. Height: 6'1". Weight: 178 lbs. Dark brown hair and dark blue eyes. At the age of twenty he made his stage debut as "Romeo" in a Hungarian production of *Romeo and Juliet* and followed it with three years of Shakespearean repertoire, Ibsen and other classics. Following the war and the political revolution in Hungary Lugosi came to New York and in 1921 organized a Hungarian dramatic company of which he was the producer, director and star. In his first production, *The Red Poppy* Lugosi played the role of a Spanish Apache and he was acclaimed by the New York critics. Then followed *Arabesque, Open House, The Devil And The Cheese.* His fifth and greatest American performance was as Count Dracula in *Dracula* at the Fulton Theater in New York City. The character of Count Dracula was regarded as one of the most difficult and dramatic roles.

His American screen career began in 1924 and his screen credits include: *The Rejected Woman, Prisoners, The Thirteenth Chair, Dracula, Black Camel, Murders In The Rue Morgue, White Zombie, Chandu The Magician, International House* and others.

His role of Count Dracula had brought him world wide fame and the latter part of his career was devoted to the "Horror" films. These horror films listed the following: *The Phantom Killer, The Wolf Man, The Ghost Of Frankenstein, The Corpse Vanishes, The Eight Men, Frankenstein Meets The Wolf Man,* etc.

Dracula,
(Universal, 1931).
He had played originally in the stage version as "Count Dracula" for over two years in New York City and the East. On tour Lugosi played eight weeks at the Biltmore, in Los Angeles, and four weeks at the Music Box in Hollywood following three return engagements to San Francisco and Oakland.

The Wolf Man, (Universal, 1941).

Black Dragons, (Monogram, 1942).
He had fulfilled his contract at Universal and moved over to the Monogram Studios who had started up a cycle of "Horror Films" and eagerly enlisted his services.

The Ape Man, (Monogram, 1943).
This film also is one of his greatest "Horror" films and the horror make-up used by Bela Lugosi was very effective in the great success of this smash hit. He was costarred in this picture with Louise Currie, Wallace Ford and Henry Hall.

Voodoo Man, (Monogram, 1944).
Bela Lugosi played the role of the Voodoo Man and he was costarred with John Carradine, Wanda McKay and George Zucco.

Idols Of Clay, (Paramount, 1920).
When Mae Murray was 21, she played the feminine lead in this picture. In this action scene we see some of the actors under contract to Paramount at that time, from left to right: Theodore Kosloff, Theodore Roberts, Elliott Dexter, Mae Murray and Edythe Chapman. Mae Murray was to do one more picture, *On With The Dance, for* Paramount.

MAE MURRAY

Born: May 10, 1898, Portsmouth, Virginia. Height: 5′2″. Weight: 115 lbs. Brown hair and blue eyes.

Educated in New York City. As a child, she took up dancing. At the age of 15 she had attracted so much attention she was selected for a place in the Ziegfeld Follies where she was found by Universal. It would be impossible for one to imagine that Mae Murray had been born anyplace but New York City. In her exotic roles on the screen she was the spirit of the Great White Way. Her screen credits include: *On With The Dance, Idols Of Clay*, at Paramount. Before her Paramount Pictures, she was starred at Universal and made *The Bride's Awakening, What Am I Bid, The Delicious Little Devil*, and *Modern Love*. She signed up with Metro, which was to become Metro-Goldwyn, and finally merged as Metro-Goldwyn-Mayer. Under this banner, she starred in *Peacock Alley, Fashion Row, Mlle. Midnight, The Merry Widow, The Masked Bride, Valencia, Altars Of Desire*, and then made a tour of the West Coast doing *The Merry Widow Waltz*. Also among her credits for M.G.M. were *Fascination, Broadway Rose, Jazzmania, The French Doll* and others.

It can be truthfully said that Mae Murray was one of the great glamour stars of the Roaring Twenties. Her parties were the talk of Hollywood. She wore the latest fashions and her gowns were the envy of all the women who saw them. Her dancing and acting created for her a faithful following of millions. She was costarred with John Gilbert in *The Merry Widow* in which she played the title role, and her performance in this spectacular is considered to be her very greatest.

In this photo we see Mae Murray posing nonchalantly with the standard equipment of all actresses: the mink coat, the roses, a new car and a chauffeur.

Mademoiselle Midnight,
(Metro, 1924).

In this scene we see her with three of her noted contemporaries and fellow actors: Robert Edison, Monte Blue and Otis Harlan. She was to marry Robert Z. Leonard, who directed this picture.

The Merry Widow,
(Metro-Goldwyn, 1925).

Mae Murray played the part of *"The Merry Widow"* with John Gilbert and Roy D'Arcy costarring. This early version was made in the silent era and was interpreted in a highly dramatic manner—a rather far cry from its original presentation as a musical. This classic skyrocketed both Mae Murray and John Gilbert to fame.

The Masked Bride,
(Metro-Goldwyn, 1925).

Mae Murray as *The Masked Bride,* costarred with that great matinee idol of the silent era, Francis X. Bushman, and Roy D'arcy who became one of the most famous arch villains in the picture industry. Mae Murray became known as "The girl with the bee stung lips."

189

DICK POWELL

DICK POWELL

Born: November 14, 1904, Mt. View, Arkansas. Died: 1963, Los Angeles, California. Height: 6'. Weight: 175 lbs. Reddish-brown hair and blue eyes.

He started as a boyish, singing emcee at the Stanley Theatre in Pittsburgh, Penna. From there he came out to Hollywood to make his screen debut as a down-and-out band leader who crooned three numbers in the picture *Blessed Event* starring Lee Tracy and Mary Brian. The vocal introduction of Dick Powell to movie audiences proved so auspicious that it started a run of movie musicals. The tenor from Mountain View, had become one of the ten top box-office names in pictures and one of the hottest singers on radio. He was a whopping success, he was making big money, and he was restless. He felt he was in a rut. He started looking for tough guy roles and eventually made a great success of this type of characterization.

His film credits include: *42nd Street; Gold Diggers of 1933; Wonder Bar; Twenty Million Sweethearts; Dames; Flirtation Walk; A Midsummer Night's Dream; Page Miss Glory; On The Avenue; I Want A Divorce; Happy Go Lucky; It Happened Tomorrow; Murder, My Sweet; Johnny O'Clock; Rogues Regiment; The Reformer And The Redhead; The Bad And The Beautiful;* and *Susan Slept Here.*

In the latter phases of his career he developed into a fine director and producer in charge of Four Star Film Productions. The greatest role of his career was in *Murder, My Sweet*, adapted from a Raymond Chandler crime story.

A Midsummer Night's Dream, (Warner Brothers, 1935).

Warner Brothers imported Max Reinhardt to help in the adaptation of this film. In the notable cast, which consisted of practically every contract player on the Warner's lot, were Dick Powell, Olivia De Havilland, James Cagney, Joe E. Brown, Jean Muir, Ross Alexander, Mickey Rooney, Anita Louise, Victor Jory, Ian Hunter, Arthur Treacher and others.

Murder, My Sweet, (R.K.O., 1944)

The ambitious Dick Powell had grown very restless under the monotony of a succession of musicals and was determined to become a serious actor. He was given the cold shoulder by his home studio, Warner Brothers, but after a series of rebuffs, he finally landed the part of a detective in a "Who-Dun-It" at R.K.O. Studios called *Murder, My Sweet.* This picture was the turning point of his career.

Shipmates Forever, (Warner Brothers, 1935).

This picture was typical of all the great musicals in which Dick Powell sang and acted. Ruby Keeler costarred with him in a majority of them. Miss Keeler was a very successful New York musical comedy actress particularly gifted in her singing and dancing. The Warner Brothers went all out to make these musicals and spared no expense in beautiful ensembles with hundreds of charming chorines with the famous Busby Berkeley supervising the choreography.

The Reformer and The Redhead, (M.G.M., 1950).

June Allyson and Dick Powell were costarred in M.G.M.'s gay, romantic comedy with David Wayne, Cecil Kellaway, Ray Collins, Robert Keith and Marvin Kaplan in the supporting roles.

Stations West, (R.K.O. Radio, 1948).

Dick Powell, Jane Greer, Guinn "Big Boy" Williams and Burl Ives starred in this great Western. The memorable scenes of the great fight between Powell and Williams could only be likened to another great fight of many years before between Tom Santchi and William Farnum in *The Spoilers.* His business arrangement with R.K.O. gave him a three-way deal as actor, director and producer.

WALLACE REID

Born: April 15, 1892, St. Louis, Missouri. Died: January 18, 1923 in Los Angeles, California. Height: 6′1″. Weight: 170 lbs. Blond hair and blue eyes.

At the age of four he played the role of a little girl in the stage play, *Slaves Of Gold*. He was the son of Hal Reid, noted playwright. When Wallace was ten years old, the Reid Family moved to New York City. He received his early education in the schools there. Afterwards, he attended the New Jersey Military Academy at Freehold. His life became a crowded one. He was a cowboy, civil engineer, reporter, motion picture director, scenario writer, stunt man, stage actor and screen celebrity. His playwright father did a vaudeville play called *The Girl And The Ranger* and Wallace accepted a part in it. After he did bits, played character parts and leads, and learned to operate a motion picture camera. From Selig's, he joined up with Biograph and went on to play the role of the Blacksmith in Griffith's *Birth Of A Nation* and in 1915 joined Paramount as a leading man, where he remained and achieved stardom by the time he was 25 years old.

His tragic, untimely death came in 1923, at the age of 31. In his six years of stardom with Paramount he made some of the greatest box-office successes rivaling the efforts of such contemporaries as Rudolph Valentino, Gloria Swanson, Elliott Dexter and Thomas Meighan.

Photo showing Wallace Reid and his wife about 1916 in their Drawing Room. Wallace Reid was unusually fond of children, and he kept quite a few animal pets. One of his greatest hobbies was music, and he had grown proficient in several instruments. He worked with some of the most distinguished character actors under the Paramount banner such as: Theodore Roberts, Theodore Kosloff, Charles Ogle, Otis Harlan and Clarence Burton.

Rimrock Jones, (Paramount, 1918).

The great majority of Wally Reid's films were action-packed and of a light, gay tempo. They were of high morals, never sexy. In this scene we see him at the bar "rolling his own," with either Duke's Mixture or that "X" Brand. At the extreme right is Charles Ogle, one of Paramount's finest character actors of the silent era. Wallace Reid had a boyish, ingratiating quality to his acting that brought him to immediate stardom.

The Crackman's Christmas, (Universal, 1916).

In the early days of the silent motion picture producers and directors sometimes found it unnecessary to use a script and often made up the situations and the story as they went along. In this scene we see Dorothy Davenport, the feminine lead, costarring with Wallace Reid. Wallace Reid produced this melodrama; Dorothy Davenport became his wife in real life.

Early Silent Drama, (Approximately 1919).

In the many years he starred for Paramount he had as his leading ladies such noted stars under contract to Paramount as: Kathlyn Williams, Lois Wilson, Eileen Percy, Wanda Hawley and many others. In this action-packed fight scene we see Wallace Reid as he emerges the victor in one of his starring features for Paramount around the year of 1919.

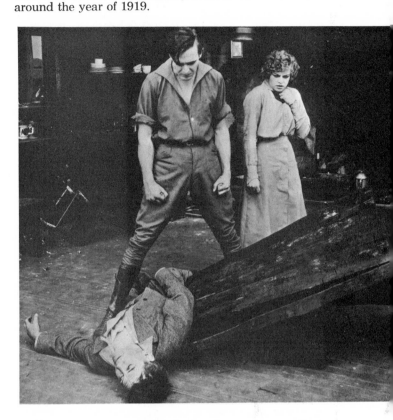

The Affairs Of Anatol, (Paramount, 1921).

In 1921 Cecil B. De Mille produced and directed this picture with Wallace Reid costarring with Gloria Swanson, then at the very pinnacle of her career.

WILL ROGERS

Born: November 4, 1879, Colagah, U.S. Cherokee Indian Territory. Died: August 15, 1935, Point Barrow, Alaska. Height: 5′ 11″. Weight: 180 lbs. with dark brown-gray streaked hair and blue eyes.

He was educated at the Willie Hassell School at Noosho, Missouri and at the Kemper Military Academy at Booneville, Missouri. He learned to rope and ride while he was a ranch hand in Oklahoma, and became a cow puncher when he was 17 years old. He went to South America and from there got a job on a cattle boat transporting mules from Buenos Aires to South Africa for British troops engaged in the Boer War. He grew homesick and took passage for New York and back to Oklahoma. He then joined another Wild West Show in Oklahoma and started on a tour of the Southwest.

By this time his rope-spinning act had attained considerable notice and an alert booking agent signed him as one of the many attractions of the 1905 annual horse show at Madison Square Garden in New York City. He was an immediate hit and was soon in demand by all booking agents. After several tours of the big time vaudeville circuits, he was finally induced to join Ziegfeld's Follies and later was featured in "Night Frolics." While he was a star performer with Ziegfeld he introduced a line of patter with his rope and pony act. In 1919 he abandoned the stage and made a series of silent pictures for Hal Roach. In 1922 he returned to the Follies and remained on Broadway until 1929 when the advent of talking pictures brought him back to the screen in *They Had To See Paris*, a Fox Film Corporation production. This picture launched him into his great screen career under the Fox banner.

His screen credits include the following silent films, made for Hal Roach Studios: *Two Wagons, Both Covered; Doubling For Romeo; Boys Will Be Boys; Family Fits; Jubilo, Jr.; Our Congressmen;*

WILL ROGERS

Going To Congress; Gee Whiz, Genevieve; and *A Texas Steer*. After his great success in *They Had To See Paris*, he also did the following productions for Fox Films: *So This Is London, Lightnin', A Connecticut Yankee, Young As You Feel, Business and Pleasure, Ambassador Bill, Down To Earth, Too Busy to Work, State Fair, David Harum, Doctor Bull, Mr. Skitch, Judge Priest, Life Begins At Forty, The County Chairman, Steamboat Round The Bend,* and *In Old Kentucky*, his last film.

A Connecticut Yankee, (Fox, 1931).
This film was adapted from Mark Twain's immortal classic. Will Rogers played the title role with Myrna Loy costarring and Maureen O'Sullivan and Frank Albertson in the supporting roles. Will Rogers' hobby became flying, and he never took a train, a boat or an automobile if he could secure an airplane for a journey of any distance. He was a warm friend of the Lindberghs and was on intimate terms with Kings and Queens in Europe and captains of industry in the United States.

194

State Fair, (Fox, 1933).

Will Rogers costarred with Janet Gaynor and Lew Ayres furnishing the love interest. They headed a notable cast which included Louise Dresser, Frank Craven, Sally Eilers and Norman Foster.

David Harum, (Fox, 1934).

In this famous old classic Will Rogers played the part of David Harum. Evelyn Venable was his feminine lead and Louis Dresser and Kent Taylor played the supporting roles with Stepin Fetchit furnishing the comedy relief. In the latter phases of his career Rogers became a correspondent for a syndicate of 200 newspapers, and carried a typewriter wherever he went.

In Old Kentucky, (Fox, 1935)

This was a fine story of race horses, race tracks and racing men in old Kentucky. Will Rogers played the part of a race horse trainer. Bill Robinson, the great dancer and comedian, played a very fine part in this, Will Rogers' final film. After the completion of this film, Will Rogers and Wiley Post, the noted aviator, started out on a flight which ended fatally at Point Barrow, Alaska.

The County Chairman, (Fox, 1935).

In this picture we had a prime example of what happens when an "irresistible force meets an immovable object," in the persons of Will Rogers and Mickey Rooney. They were aided in their many situations by Berton Churchill, one of the finest character actors of his time.

NORMA TALMADGE

Born: May 26, 1897, Niagara Falls, New York.
Died: December 24, 1957, Las Vegas, Nevada.
Height: 5'4". Weight: 108 lbs. Brown hair and brown eyes.

She was educated in the public and high schools of Brooklyn, New York. Her first screen work was with Vitagraph in 1914, and in the sixteen years that followed she was to work for D. W. Griffith, First National Studios, United Artists, and in that time she played in everything from one-reelers to full features. Basically, she had attained her screen fame as a great motion picture star of the silent era, but she continued to be very successful and big box office with the advent of the talkies. Her greatest successes were made under the banner of the United Artists Productions. It would be impossible to historically record all the films in which she played, but the following titles are considered her greatest: *The Tale Of Two Cities, Salome, Sunshine And Shadows, The Battle Cry Of Peace*, for D. W. Griffith. She made the following: *Missing Links, The Children In The House, Going Straight*, and *The Devil's Needle*. For Selznick from 1917 to 1920 she made: *Panthea, Poppy, The Moth, Ghosts Of Yesterday*, and *Her Only Way*. Under her contract to First National she played in many, many great pictures, and in the latter part of her career she worked for United Artists in *The Dove, The Woman Disputed, New York Nights* and *Du Barry*, in 1930.

Norma Talmadge mixed her beauty and personality with brains; in addition to her great success as a topflight motion picture star, she was also noted for her very successful real estate investments. She had entered pictures at the age of fourteen years without any previous experience and had developed into a glamorous dramatic actress of the highest magnitude.

NORMA TALMADGE

Branded Woman,
(First National, 1920).
This film was among the first of a very long series of productions that Norma Talmadge made for First National. In this scene Miss Talmadge is shown in the slave market as the eager native buyers enter into spirited bidding to add her to their harems.

196

Kiki, (First National, 1926).
Norma Talmadge created one of her greatest successes in her role of "Kiki." She had come a long way from her first acting stint at Vitagraph when she was paid $25 a week. Twenty-five years later she was to receive as much as $250,000 for a film and to head her own independent production unit.

Untitled Norma Talmadge-Eugene O'Brien Photoplay
Norma Talmadge and Eugene O'Brien proved to be a very successful combination. Joseph Schenck, her husband at that time, was given much credit for Norma's success. He selected her scripts and attended to the assignment of talent and directors to her films. Even after their divorce Norma still continued to accept Schenck's advice in all her business matters, and they remained the best of friends.

Camille, (First National, 1927). Gilbert Roland was an extra when Miss Talmadge picked him for the leading role of Armand in *Camille*, after seeing some test rushes of the young latin actor. Norma Talmadge brought a new interpretation of *Camille* to the screen and in this scene we see the two stars in one of their exotic love scenes.

The Dove, (United Artists, 1928). The story of *The Dove* was laid in a mythical land. In this scene we see the grand old veteran the most unscrupulous villain of them all, Noah Beery, as he plies his machinations upon his unsuspecting victim, Norma Talmadge.

TYRONE POWER

Born: May 5, 1913, Cincinnati, Ohio. Died: 1958 on location in Spain. Height: 6'. Weight: 115 lbs. Dark brown hair and brown eyes.

Tyrone Power was the third generation carrying the name of Tyrone Power to theatrical fame. He was perpetuating a dramatic dynasty that was founded by his great-grandfather on the Dublin stage in 1827.

His great-grandfather, Tyrone Power I, was a celebrated Irish Comedian named after County Tyrone, and his father, Tyrone II, was for years a commanding luminary of the American Stage, renowned for his superb Shakespearean characterizations. The youthful actor with the dark brown eyes and sudden, confiding smile was acutely aware of the responsibility he bore to his profession. He maintained with grace and dignity the traditions that were his birthright.

He had been a top box-office star since he emerged as an overnight sensation in *Lloyds Of London* in 1936.

His early education started when he was sent to St. Xavier Academy where he completed his elementary schoolwork. From there he went to the Preparatory School of The University Of Dayton, in Dayton, Ohio.

Tyrone Power, Sr. had been engaged for a short season in Shakespearean Repertoire for the early fall of 1931. He decided to give his son an opportunity. He took Tyrone to a quiet summer retreat in Quebec. There, during the summer of 1931 under the direction of his father, recognized as one of the greatest actors in theatrical history, the boy was given intensive study and rehearsals.

At the conclusion of the Chicago season, Mr. Power, was engaged to go to Hollywood to play the starring role in Paramount's spoken production of *The Miracle Man*. Tyrone went to Hollywood also as he had been promised a small part in a play. The father and son were living together in Hollywood.

Work on *The Miracle Man* was underway when Mr. Power was taken ill on the set. He made no complaint and worked until midnight. Tyrone was called and took him home. At four o'clock that morning he died in his son's arms. The small part Tyrone Jr. was to have in *The Miracle Man* did not materialize. He spent two years of heartbreak in Hollywood and then decided to go to New York City where he made the usual whirl of the casting managers' offices. His first real break came through the courtesy of Helen Mencken who arranged for an interview with the right theatrical producers.

After doing summer stock, he was placed in Catherine Cornell's production of *Romeo and Juliet* where he attracted the attention of Fox Film talent scouts. His screen credits (1936) include: *Girls' Dormitory, Ladies In Love, Lloyds of London*, (20th Century-Fox); in 1937: *Love Is News, Cafe Metropole, Thin Ice, Second Honeymoon*, (20th Century-Fox); in 1938: *In Old Chicago, Alexander's Ragtime Band*, (20th Century-Fox); *Marie Antoinette* (M.G.M.); *Suez, Jesse James*, (20th Century-Fox); in 1939: *Rose Of Washington Square, Second Fiddle, The Rains Came; Also The Black Swan, Captain From Castile, The Razor's Edge, The Black Rose, The Mark of Zorro, Prince Of Foxes, Brigham Young* and others.

In his screen career of 22 years he maintained full status as a topflight star. His sudden death in a dueling scene with George Sanders on location in Spain in 1958 was an unexpected, tragic end to a fine career.

Lloyds of London,
(20th Century-Fox, 1936).
Upon his arrival at the Fox Studio, his first two pictures were *Girls' Dormitory* and *Ladies In Love.* He was to catapult to immediate stardom and create a tremendous impact upon the feminine film fans.

Marie Antoinette,
(M.G.M., 1938).
Norma Shearer, at the M.G.M. Studios, was to play the title role in this picture. Tyrone Power was loaned out to M.G.M. by Fox Studios to co-star with her. They headed a distinguished cast which included Robert Morley, Anita Louise, Gladys George, Joseph Schildkraut and others.

The Black Swan, (20th Century-Fox, 1942).
Tyrone Power, George Sanders and Maureen
O'Hara costarred in Raphael Sabatini's lusty
tale of high piracy in the Caribbean. Included
in this cast were Anthony Quinn, Thomas Mitchell, Laird Cregar, etc., etc. In this scene we see
Tyrone Power dueling to the death with George
Sanders in 1942, totally unaware that in another
dueling scene with George Sanders on a cold
morning in Spain he was to end his life.

Blood And Sand, (20th Century-Fox, 1941).
The Fox Studios decided to do a second version of Ibanez'
famous classic of the bullfight, and Tyrone Power was costarred with Rita Hayworth and Linda Darnell. The supporting cast included Alla Nazimova, Laird Cregar, John
Carradine, Anthony Quinn and others. 20th Century-Fox
spared no expense. They filmed the bullfight scenes in
Mexico City. Alla Nazimova as the Mother begs her son
to quit the bull ring before he gets killed.

Prince Of Foxes (20th Century-Fox, 1949).
This picture was directed by that veteran director, Henry King. The story was taken from Samuel Shellabarger's novel and depicted the family
of Borgia in their political machinations, intrigue
and diabolical elimination of opponents. Tyrone
Power, Orson Welles, Wanda Hendrix and Everett Sloane costarred.

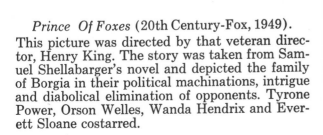

201

C. AUBREY SMITH

Born: July 21, 1863, London, England. Died: 1948.

His motion picture career began at the age of 48. Had motion pictures come into earlier prominence as a medium of entertainment, this British character actor undoubtedly would have made his cinema debut in his thirties instead of his late forties. Years before he ever faced a movie camera he was an internationally renowned actor, a mainstay of the New York and London stages. During his years with the screen, Smith had seen the character actor steadily rise from semi-obscurity to a position of importance in the industry. His own portrayals had aided immeasurably in this advancement of the character players' estate.

As a youth, he was educated at Charterhouse School, then entered Cambridge with the intention of becoming a physician.

At Cambridge he got his first taste of theatricals, playing with the University's Amateur Dramatic Club. In 1892 he made his first professional stage debut on a provincial tour with the Tapping and Cartwright Company.

Through the years that followed, he appeared with the outstanding stars of England and America, and was featured or starred in some 76 plays, including contemporary successes and Shakespearean classics.

The famous actors and actresses with whom he appeared included Ellen Terry, Sir John Hare, Sir Johnston Forbes Robertson, Mrs. Pat Campbell, Cyril Maude, Grace George, Sir Charles Hawtrey, Billie Burke, Maude Adams and Ethel Barrymore.

His screen credits include: *The Prisoner of Zenda, Little Lord Fauntleroy, Garden Of Allah, Romeo and Juliet, Lloyds Of London, Wee Willie Winkie, China*

C. AUBREY SMITH

Seas, Lives Of A Bengal Lancer, Clive Of India, The Scarlet Empress, Morning Glory, The House of Rothschild, Trader Horn, and others.

He learned to play the crabby father, scheming uncle, middle-aged villain and kindly old man. His role in *The Hurricane* as "Father Paul," the aged priest, is considered to be one of his outstanding characterizations.

The House Of Rothschild, (United Artists, 1934). In this scene we see Baron Rothschild, played by George Arliss, toasting the victorious General, played by C. Aubrey Smith. This picture had a very distinguished cast consisting of Loretta Young, Robert Young, Helen Westley and Boris Karloff.

The Crusades,
(Cecil B. De Mille—Paramount, 1935). This picture was one of Cecil B. De Mille's great biblical spectaculars. Loretta Young costarred with Henry Wilcoxon, C. Henry Gordon, C. Aubrey Smith and many others. In his screen career C. Aubrey Smith had played character parts in approximately 50 features. In his years on the American Screen he had played with all the great stars in the years from the 1930's to the late 1940's.

Little Lord Fauntleroy,
(United Artists, 1936).
In this great old English classic Freddie
Bartholomew played the title role with
C. Aubrey Smith playing the part of
the uncle. The outstanding cast consisted of Dolores Costello, Guy Kibbee
and Mickey Rooney. David O. Selznick
produced.

The Garden Of Allah,
(United Artists, 1936).
David O. Selznick produced
this picture and costarred were
Marlene Dietrich, Charles
Boyer, Joseph Schildkraut and
C. Aubrey Smith.

The Hurricane, (United Artists, 1937).
(A Samuel Goldwyn Production).
In this scene we see C. Aubrey Smith,
Raymond Massey, Mary Astor,
Thomas Mitchell and Jerome Cowan
who played the outstanding leads with
Dorothy Lamour and Jon Hall starring.
C. Aubrey Smith's portrayal of the
aged priest in the midst of a great trop-
ical catastrophe was one of his greatest
characterizations.

LEWIS STONE

Born: November 15, 1879, Worcester, Massachusetts. Died: 1953 in California. Height: 5'10½". Weight: 165 lbs. Gray hair and hazel eyes.

He received his early education in Worcester and graduated from the Bernard School in New York, finishing his studies just in time to enlist in the Army for the Spanish-American War.

It was right after his war service that Stone made his stage debut, substituting for a man who became ill while *Sidetracked* was being presented in New York. Stone's performance so impressed the manager that he remained in the cast.

After starring in Broadway productions, Stone went to Los Angeles and became the matinee idol of the old Belasco Stock Company under John Blackwood's managership. His first screen role was with Bessie Barriscale in *Honor's Altar* filmed by Thomas H. Ince. He was then placed under contract with First National where he did several notable films, signed a long-term contract with Metro-Goldwyn-Mayer shortly before the advent of talking pictures. He successfully made the transition between the Silent Era and the "Talkies." Included in his screen credits are: *Scaramouche, Don Juan's Three Nights, The Blonde Saint, The Private Life Of Helen Of Troy.* For M.G.M. he worked in *A Woman Of Affairs, The Trial Of Mary Dugan, Madame X, Their Own Desire, The Big House, The Secret Six, Inspiration, Mata Hari, Grand Hotel, The White Sister,* and many others.

He had been an officer in the American Army in two wars, a colonel in the Chinese Army, stage idol, and distinguished aristocrat of the screen. From his years in the military he had acquired an imposing military figure, and his many years on the stage had given him the necessary experience to become very successful.

LEWIS STONE

Son Daughter, (M.G.M., 1932). Lewis Stone played the part of an ancient Chinese aristocrat with Helen Hayes in the leading feminine role. At any time it would be very difficult for a Caucasian to play Chinese roles, but Lewis Stone, with his many years of stage training, and Helen Hayes, with her great New York stage successes behind her, enacted them superbly.

Mata Hari, (M.G.M., 1932).

In this famous war story of the international spy, Greta Garbo played the title role and Lewis Stone was very effective as the sinister leader of the spy organization who directed her activities. Ramon Novarro and Lionel Barrymore were also costarred in this picture.

David Copperfield, (M.G.M., 1935).

In this English classic M.G.M. selected a memorable, cast. In this scene we see Lewis Stone, Frank Lawton and Roland Young. Freddie Bartholomew played the part of "David Copperfield" and Edna May Oliver with W. C. Fields supplied the comedy relief. Basil Rathbone gave a very fine performance in his supporting role.

Grand Hotel, (M.G.M., 1932).

Edmund Goulding, one of the better British directors, directed this picture, and M.G.M. created a spectacular. A distinguished cast included Joan Crawford, Wallace Beery, Greta Garbo, Lionel Barrymore, John Barrymore and Lewis Stone. This picture and its film adaptation was taken from Vicki Baum's best-selling book of the same name.

Out West With The Hardys, (M.G.M., 1938).

The "Judge Hardy" series became one of the most successful features at M.G.M. In this scene we see the typical American family. From left to right are Cecilia Parker, Mickey Rooney, Fay Holden, Lewis Stone, Sara Haden and Virginia Weidler.

Old San Francisco, (Warner Bros., 1927).
Warner Oland costarred with Dolores Costello with Anna May Wong in the supporting role. Warner Oland had made a very successful career in depicting the wily oriental. From these villainous roles he was to do the "Charlie Chan" mystery series.

ANNA MAY WONG

Born: January 3, 1907, Los Angeles, California. Died: February 3, 1961, Los Angeles, California. Height: 5′4″½. Weight: 120 lbs. Blue-black hair and brown eyes.

Educated in Hollywood, California. At an early age she was noticed by the picture people and began doing small parts.

She quickly graduated into many of the big productions that were based upon stories of China and the Orient. She developed into a very beautiful actress and became in great demand in many of the Chinese mystery productions. Her screen credits include: *Old San Francisco, Across To Singapore, Chinatown Charlie, Toll Of The Sea, Mr. Wu, The Thief Of Bagdad, Daughter Of The Dragon, Shanghai Express, Daughter Of Shanghai* and many many others.

Her role in *The Shanghai Express* is considered to be the best part of her career.

Daughter Of The Dragon, (Paramount, 1931).
Anna May Wong, Warner Oland and Sessue Hayakawa were costarred in this story of the Orient. At the height of her career she went to Europe and appeared in English and German Productions for three years. On her return to the United States she was put under contract to Paramount and her first picture was *Daughter Of The Dragon*.

Shanghai Express,
(Paramount, 1932).
Marlene Dietrich starred with Clive Brook, Anna May Wong and Warner Oland costarring. This picture was directed by Josef von Sternberg, the great German director.

Dangerous To Know, (Paramount, 1938).
Gail Patrick, Anna May Wong, Akim Tamiroff, Roscoe Karns, Porter Hall, Lloyd Nolan, Anthony Quinn and Harvey Stephens comprised the cast of this picture with Akim Tamiroff playing a very villainous part.

Daughter Of Shanghai, (Paramount, 1937).
After the success pattern of *Shanghai Express* Paramount followed several years later with *The Daughter Of Shanghai,* featuring an exceptionally fine cast including Anna May Wong, Philip Ahn, Charles Bickford, Anthony Quinn, Larry Crabbe, Cecil Cunningham, J. Carrol Naish and Ching Wah Lee.

JEAN HERSHOLT

Born: July 12, 1886, Copenhagen, Denmark. Height: 5'11". Weight: 185 lbs. Black hair and dark blue eyes. Died: 1956.

He was the son of Henry and Claire Hersholt, famous actor and actress, then leading artists at the Royal Theater. Graduating from high school, he attended the Copenhagen Art School where he was a star pupil. In the meantime he had become interested in the stage, and took dramatic lessons from actors of his acquaintance. Finally, he passed the entrance examination and was made a student actor at the Dagmar Theater where he served a 2½ year apprenticeship. His parents reconciled themselves to the idea, and Jean became a full-fledged actor. In 1914, Danes in America who admired his work, invited him to this country to appear in Danish plays and lecture on the Drama.

The Danish engagement at San Francisco was concluded at about the time picture studios were beginning to assume importance in Hollywood. The Hersholts went to Los Angeles. Jean Hersholt received his screen experience at Inceville, and from there he graduated to the old Triangle Studios.

In 1916-17 he was under contract at Universal. He and the late Lon Chaney shared the same room, carrying out experiments in make-up. His biggest break came when Mary Pickford, preparing to star in *Tess Of The Storm Country*, insisted that he play an important role in her picture. The role in the Pickford picture attracted the attention of Erich von Stroheim, then casting *Greed*. He was soon hailed as one of the really great character actors of the day. His picture credits include: *The Painted Veil, Cat And The Fiddle, The Old Soak, Beast Of The City, Sins Of Man, Seventh Heaven, Men In White, Dinner At Eight, Grand Hotel, Hell's Harbor, Trans-Atlantic, Private Lives, The Country Doctor, One In A Million, Heidi,* and others.

He devoted a large part of his life to many civic projects and was a generous philanthropist.

Princess Virtue, (Universal-Bluebird, 1916).
This picture was made in the very early phases of Jean Hersholt's career. He costarred with Mae Murray. He did several pictures for Universal, and from this studio he was to be placed under contract to the Mary Pickford company and costar with her in *Tess Of The Storm Country*. This was to be the turning of his career.

Christopher Bean, (M.G.M., 1933).
Jean Hersholt was costarred with Marie Dressler, one of America's greatest character actresses. This film was follow-up of *Emma* in which Dressler and Hersholt also costarred.

Sins Of Man,
(20th Century Fox, 1936).
Jean Hersholt starred with a supporting cast which included Don Ameche, Allen Jenkins, J. Edward Bromberg and Ann Shoemaker. Jean Hersholt had also become well known for his famous collection of first editions rated as one of the most important in the country. He also had a fine collection of rare paintings.

Greed, (Metro-Goldwyn, 1924).
Erich von Stroheim, at the very peak of his directorial career, called upon him for a character role in *Greed.* This particular film required the services of Zasu Pitts, Gibson Gowland, Chester Conklin and Jean Hersholt.

Heidi, (20th Century Fox, 1937).
Shirley Temple, the world's greatest child star at the peak of her acting career was cast in the title role. Jean Hersholt led a distinguished cast which included Arthur Treacher, Helen Westley, Pauline Moore, Thomas Beck, Mary Nash, Sidney Blackmer and Mady Christians.

209

ERICH VON STROHEIM

Born: September 22, 1885, Vienna, Austria. Died: May 12, 1957, Paris, France.

Educated in an Austrian Military Academy. Misfortune overtook his family in 1909, and von Stroheim came to America. He immediately applied for naturalization. The world of make-believe had a strong appeal for him, and between his varied and numerous jobs, he wrote a vaudeville sketch. Then, this new and wonderful invention — the motion picture camera — beckoned him to Los Angeles in 1914. In Hollywood, he worked as an extra when he could find work, but because of his nationality, the engagements were few. For two years and a half he lived a hand-to-mouth existence, walking back and forth from Los Angeles to Hollywood when he was playing in pictures and usually going without lunch. He was on the point of giving up, when he was engaged as Assistant Director for John Emerson. He had his first really big opportunity, however, in playing German and Austrian Officers after this country had gone into the war.

In Griffith's *Hearts Of The World* and Holubar's *Heart Of Humanity* he played important roles. When the war was over, he was inactive for nine months because of the dearth of war pictures. Then, he directed, starred and wrote *Blind Husbands* for Universal. Then he did *The Wedding March* for Famous. He starred in *The Great Gabbo*, a James Cruze Production. His screen credits include: *Three Faces East, Friends And Lovers, Lost Squadron, As You Desire Me*, and many, many others. The preceding films were the ones in which he acted. The following films were the ones that he directed: *The Devil's*

ERICH VON STROHEIM

Passkey, Foolish Wives, Merry-Go-Round, Greed, The Merry Widow, Tempest among others.

In the latter phases of his great career, von Stroheim devoted himself purely to acting, his later pictures were: *Five Graves To Cairo, North Star, Storm Over Lisbon, The Great Flammarion, Scotland Yard Inspector* and *Sunset Boulevard*.

The Wedding March, (Paramount, 1928).

This scene perfectly illustrates the early career of Erich von Stroheim, as we see him in the splendid dress uniform of a Prussian Officer with Sidney Bracy, one of the great supporting stars of the silent days playing the part of his orderly. His military bearing and experience were natural for this part.

The Great Gabbo,
(A James Cruze Production, 1929).

In this film von Stroheim played the part of a ventriloquist who developed hallucinations about his dummy, and the resulting situations created a superb theatrical fantasy.

As You Desire Me, (M.G.M., 1932).
The Great Garbo was the star of this picture, but
von Stroheim's work was quite exceptional, and
in this scene we see a romantic interlude between
von Stroheim and Garbo. This scene seems to portray von Stroheim as the predatory male with
Garbo in complete silent submission.

Five Graves To Cairo, (Paramount, 1943).
Erich von Stroheim returns to the screen as Field
Marshall Erwin Rommel of Germany's Afrika Korps
in Paramount's *Five Graves To Cairo*. Left to right
are Fortunio Bonanova, Franchot Tone, Fred Nur-
ney, von Stroheim, Konstantin Shayle and Peter
Van Eyck. Setting of the film is the North African
Desert. Von Stroheim struck the spark of acting
genius, and in the part of Rommel did the finest performance of his entire career.

Sunset Boulevard, (Paramount, 1950).
In this scene we see the immortal Gloria Swanson
with William Holden, Nancy Olson and Erich von
Stroheim in this dramatic story of frustration, ambition and romance in Hollywood. Von Stroheim
played the part of a chauffeur.

HENRY B. WALTHALL

Born: 1878 at Shelby City, Alabama. Died: June, 1936. Height: 5'7". Weight: 130 lbs. Gray hair and brown eyes.

As a youth he had acquired some stage experience and entered motion pictures in the year of 1910. He made himself a permanent part of motion picture history when he joined up with D. W. Griffith and worked in *Birth Of A Nation*. Included among his screen credits were: *The Scarlet Letter, Freedom Of The Press, Wings, Abraham Lincoln, The Payoff*, (Vitaphone, 1932); *The Sin Of Nora Moran*, and in 1934, *Viva Villa*, (M.G.M.). *Men In White* (M.G.M.); *Judge Priest* (Fox); *A Tale Of Two Cities* (M.G.M.); and his last picture was *The Garden Murder Case*, (M.G.M., 1936).

In the latter phases of his career he played supporting roles and became a very noted character actor. He was in great demand as the kindly uncle, grandfather and fathers of the various leads. From his first picture in 1910 until his death in 1936, he had worked in every type of film role and done them exceptionally well. He had many fine screen credits to his name, and the great majority of his parts were notable and outstanding, but he had immortalized himself forever upon the public consciousness in D. W. Griffith's *Birth Of A Nation* (1915) in which he played a soldier of the Confederacy affectionately called "The Little Colonel."

HENRY B. WALTHALL

Birth Of A Nation, (D. W. Griffith, 1915). D. W. Griffith's memorable classic on the Civil War gave Henry B. Walthall his greatest role. In this scene we see Henry B. Walthall at the close of the Civil War, as he returns to the ancestral plantation and once again meets Mae Marsh.

Road To Mandalay, (M.G.M., 1926).

This picture was a starring vehicle for Lon Chaney; Henry B. Walthall played the part of a priest and Lois Moran the role of his ward. Henry B. Walthall stood out clearly as one of our great film pioneers. The artistry and individuality of this star early caused him to become known as the "Mansfield" of the screen, a well-earned title.

Speakeasy,
(Fox, 1929, 100% dialogue Fox Movietone Feature). It was a far cry from the early days of *The Birth Of A Nation* to the early days of the talkies. We see him in this scene with Warren Hymer in a 100% talking Fox picture.

Dante's Inferno, (Fox, 1935).

Spencer Tracy and Claire Trevor costarred with Henry B. Walthall and Alan Dinehart played the supporting roles. Henry B. Walthall played the part of a carnival proprietor of a side show attraction called *Dante's Inferno* and Claire Trevor was his daughter. Spencer Tracy as an unemployed stoker shows them the way to riches and success.

A Tale Of Two Cities, (M.G.M., 1935).

Henry B. Walthall played the part of Dr. Manette in this historical classic. The picture costarred Ronald Colman, Elizabeth Allen, Reginald Owen, Basil Rathbone and Edna May Oliver.

WARREN WILLIAM

Born: December 2, 1896, Aitken, Minnesota. Died: North Hollywood, California, 1948.

Warren William's greatest full success occurred when he was under contract to Warner Brothers, but before this happened, at the outbreak of the First World War, Warren William joined the Army and went to France. After the Armistice was signed, he remained in France and joined up with a theatrical troupe which was touring the Army Camps. Although young William had no stage experience, he was the type for the leading role in *Under Cover*. Soldier audiences liked his acting, and when he came back to America, he decided to see a few Broadway managers in an effort to secure acting roles. He got the Richard Dix role in the road company of *I Love You*. Soon came a Broadway chance in *Expressing Willie* and Warren William's personality began to register with Broadway managers and audiences. He became very successful as a leading man on the New York Stage and was readily persuaded to answer the call to talking pictures. His first picture was *Expensive Women* in which he played opposite Dolores Costello. Among his screen credits was *Twelve Miles Out*. He played Francine Larrimore's husband in *Let Us Be Gay*, and *Those Who Love*.

His early career records the following pictures: *The Honor Of The Family* with Bebe Daniels; *The Woman From Monte Carlo* opposite Lil Dagover, the German actress; *Under Eighteen* and *Beauty And The Boss* opposite Marion Marsh; *The Dark Horse, The Mouthpiece, The Match King, Employees' Entrance, The Mind Reader, Golddiggers Of 1933*. He also did several of the Erle Stanley Gardner murder mysteries such as *The Case Of The Howling Dog, The Case Of The Curious Bride, The Case Of The Lucky Legs* and *The Case Of The Velvet Claws*, and many, many others.

A hitherto unpublished and practically unknown chapter of his theatrical youth is the fact that he played the male lead in *The Perils Of Pauline* with Pearl White in some of her serials, and thus his theatrical-film career covered the years of 1914 to 1946. In the Warner Brothers Films, where he did his most outstanding work, he played the role of smart lawyers and also criminal investigators.

Cleopatra, (Paramount, 1934).
(A Cecil B. De Mille Production).
Claudette Colbert played the title role with Warren William playing the part of Julius Caesar, and Henry Wilcoxon enacted the role of Marc Anthony. Cecil B. De Mille produced and directed this production and created a masterpiece with his ability to combine the lavish splendor of his great sets and the projection of the finest theatrical personalities of his time.

Madame X, (M.G.M., 1937).

Gladys George, who had made a great dramatic success on the New York Stage, played the title role in this film with John Beal playing the part of the Lawyer Son, and Reginald Owen and Warren William were in the supporting cast. Pauline Frederick had done a silent version, Ruth Chatterton had also done a version, and this Gladys George version proved to be a big box-office success.

The Mouthpiece, (Warner Brothers, 1932).

In this scene Warren William, playing the part of the Defense Attorney, proves the point he was trying to make by completely knocking out the prize fighter, played by Stanley Fields, in this picture. These unorthodox methods of proving a legal point would do very well in a film courtroom, but in real life they would quickly be declared irrelevant and immaterial and thrown out of the records. Another amazing point about these courtroom scenes was the Prosecuting Attorney's strange silence while the Defense Attorney indulged in all these wild antics.

Imitation Of Life, (Universal, 1934).

Claudette Colbert and a superb male star were well met in this picture — both of them at the height and pinnacle of their respective careers.

The Man In The Iron Mask, (United Artists, 1939).

This picture was one of the many swashbuckling tales in which Louis Hayward excelled. Joan Bennett played the feminine lead and Warren William also costarred. Warren William, with his many years and experience on the New York Stage, had acquired the ability to project his personality into any type of role demanded of him, and as a result, he was in great demand by the studios.

215

An Early Keystone Comedy of 1912—Mabel Normand and The Mack Sennett Company. At the extreme left we see Mabel Normand playing the part of a Princess with the entire Mack Sennett company participating in the evolution of the "gag" situations. A good majority of the still photos portraying the Mack Sennett history reveal the mechanics of the gag.

MABEL NORMAND

Born: Nov. 10, 1898, Boston, Massachusetts. Died: February 24, 1930, Los Angeles, California. Height: 5' 3". Weight; 120 lbs. Black hair and brown eyes.

She was educated at St. Mary's Convent at North Westport, Mass. She entered motion pictures in New York in 1910 at the age of sixteen and played her first screen roles for the old Vitagraph and Biograph companies. From the beginning of her career she was cast in comedy roles. It was while she was employed at the Biograph Studio that she first met Mack Sennett, under whose direction she was destined to achieve world-wide fame. Sennett himself was a struggling film actor in those days and David Griffith was only beginning to attract attention as. a director.

D. W. Griffith signed her up and brought the Biograph Company to Los Angeles. She became Queen of the Sennett Lot among such actresses as Gloria Swanson, Louise Fazenda, Marie Prevost, Phyllis Haver and Polly Moran.

The famous actors and comedians on the lot were Wallace Beery, Charles Chaplin, Chester Conklin, Ben Turpin. Mabel Normand and Roscoe "Fatty" Arbuckle costarred in *Mabel and Fatty* series of comedies. One of her greatest pictures on the Sennett Lot was *Tillie's Punctured Romance*, but her greatest role came when she played the title part of *Mickey*.

After *Mickey*, Sam Goldwyn signed her up for $3,500 a week which was the largest salary paid in motion pictures up to that time. When her Goldwyn contract was up, she went back to Sennett and made three of the outstanding comedies of her career: *Molly O, Suzanna,* and *The Extra Girl.* In the late 1920's she contracted tuberculosis which led to her death in 1930.

An Early Keystone Comedy Circa 1913—
Title Unknown

Before he became a producer and built his own studio, Mack Sennett was one of the slapstick actors, and, incidentally, one of the very best. In this scene we see again the gag situation with Mack Sennett, Mabel Normand and Alice Davenport all participating to build up the usual disastrous conclusion.

Mickey,
(Mack Sennett Comedy, 1918).
This full-length feature comedy immortalized Mabel Normand in screen history. As she romped through these scenes, she brought out that tomboyish quality of her personality, and all those who viewed the picture knew that Mabel Normand and "Mickey" were one and the same. This picture also was known as Mack Sennett's "Mortgage Lifter." Rumored to be in financial difficulties, the success of this film enabled him to continue production. In this scene we see Minnie, the old Indian woman, and Mabel Normand in a tender moment.

My Valet,
(Triangle, 1915, Mack Sennett Keystone Comedy).
In this story Mabel Normand and Mack Sennett co-starred, and Raymond Hitchcock, that very fine musical comedy star from the New York Stage, played the title role. Mabel Normand, off-screen, was a vivacious, intelligent young woman. She was noted for her open-handed generosity, and many a friend who expressed a liking for any bric-a-brac in her house suddenly found themselves the owner of the mentioned article.

The Slim Princess,
(Samuel Goldwyn, 1920).
At the conclusion of *Mickey* Mabel left the Sennett lot and signed up with Samuel Goldwyn at the unheard of sum of $3,500 a week. She made *Sis Hopkins* and others for Sam Goldwyn.

SLIM SUMMERVILLE

Born: Albuquerque, New Mexico, July 10, 1892. Died: Jan. 5, 1946. Height: 6' 2½". Weight: 160 lbs. Brown hair and brown eyes.

His mother died when he was five years old and his father took him to live at Chatham, Canada, where he received his early education. When he was ten, Slim was sent to live with an aunt in Oklahoma, but his spirit was too adventurous to be tied to a school desk. He eventually ran away to make his fortune, and for six years he knocked about the United States, Canada and Mexico. He rode the rods over practically every railroad of the country.

In 1913, when he was "on the bum" just turned eighteen, Slim found his way to Los Angeles, where he planned to visit an uncle. He couldn't find his uncle, and he worked for six months as a pool-room porter washing out cuspidors and racking up balls.

He became acquainted with Edgar Kennedy, a slapstick comedian at the Mack Sennett Studios. Through the good offices of Kennedy, Slim secured work at the studio for the princely sum of $3.50 a day.

Slim became a fixture on the Keystone Police Force, and Sennett offered him the astounding guarantee of four working days a week for $12.00. Slim took it. Thereafter, the astute Sennett featured Slim in a series of comedies. Eventually he became one of Sennett's ace directors, when a comedy was turned out in two days of shooting. But he returned to acting, and in 1930 got his greatest break—the role of "Tjaden" in *All Quiet On The Western Front* which brought him a long term contract with the Universal Studios.

His screen credits include: *The Beloved Rogue*;

SLIM SUMMERVILLE

King Of Jazz; Racing Youth; Unexpected Father; Love, Honor and Oh Baby; Life Begins At Forty with Rogers; *Jesse James* with Tyrone Power, etc.

An Early Mack Sennett Comedy, (Circa 1916-17). This era was the start of Slim Summerville's career in the days of the Mack Sennett Keystone Comedies when the directors were turning them out at the rate of one two-reeler every two days. In this scene we see Bobby Dunn with Juanita Hansen and Slim Summerville going through the gags and situations of the Mack Sennett Comedy.

The Beloved Rogue, (United Artists, 1927).
The producers, with a real stroke of genius, brought John Barrymore, fresh from his successful stage career, to play the part of Francois Villon, the revolutionary French Poet, and Mack Swain along with Slim Summerville were given roles of his cronies in this great film.

All Quiet On The Western Front, (Universal, 1930).
Erich Remarque, the great German author, had written a best-selling novel on the German side of the war in *All Quiet On The Western Front*. Lew Ayres starred. Slim Summerville, Ben Alexander, Louis Wolheim and Raymond Griffith were among the great cast. The highlight of the picture shows Slim Summerville and Lew Ayres in some comedy by-play during their training period.

White Fang, (Fox, 1936).
Slim Summerville, Charles Winninger, Michael Whalen, Jean Muir and John Carradine comprised the cast of this dog story of the great Northwest. Lightning, a great movie dog, played the title role of this picture. This picture was a sequel to a preceding one titled *Call Of The Wild*.

Rebecca Of Sunnybrook Farm, (Fox, 1938).
Shirley Temple played the part of "Rebecca of Sunnybrook Farm" at the age of seven. 20th Century-Fox surrounded her with a superb cast including Randolph Scott, Jack Haley, Gloria Stuart, Phyllis Brooks, Bill Robinson, Alan Dinehart and J. Edward Bromberg. In this photo we see Helen Westley looking askance at Shirley Temple with Slim Summerville as a very interested listener.

His Auto-Ruination, (Triangle Plays, 1916).
This film was made in the early days of the Mack Sennett Studios. In this sextet of comedy players we see Bobby Dunn, Julia Faye, Mack Swain, May Wells, Harry Gribbon and Harry McCoy who were all under contract with the Keystone Comedies. Mack Sennett demanded that his still photographer photograph the "gag," and as a result, the Mack Sennett photos have become collector's items.

MACK SWAIN

Born: February 16, 1876, Salt Lake City, Utah. Height: 6' 2". Weight: 280 lbs. Blond hair and green eyes.

He was educated in the public schools of Salt Lake City, Utah. He left home at an early age and had 22 years of stage training in vaudeville, minstrel, comedy-drama and musical comedy. His stage credits were *Around The World In 80 Days, Human Hearts* and *Brown's In Town*. He joined up with the Mack Sennett Company and was with them for many years. He costarred with Charles Chaplin in *The Gold Rush*. His screen credits include: *Gentlemen Prefer Blondes, Cohens And The Kellys, Mirianne*, (M.G.M.); *Cohens And The Kellys In Atlantic City*, (Universal); *The Last Warning*, (Universal); *The Beloved Rogue* (Warner Brothers), and others.

He quickly became one of the rollicking, roistering comedians of the Mack Sennett Studio. His varied theatrical experience had made him a master of the slapstick, and he was right at home in all the impossible situations that the Mack Sennett writers could dig up. His role as the food-crazed prospector who believed that Charlie Chaplin was a piece-de-resistance and was determined to make a meal out of him was one of the funniest comedy bits between Chaplin and Mack Swain and contributed greatly to the smashing success of *The Gold Rush*. In the latter phases of his career he teamed up with George Sidney to do the *Cohen And Kelly series*.

Untitled Mack Sennett Keystone Comedy, (Circa 1916-1920).
In this scene we see Dora Rogers attempting to seduce Mack Swain. Mack Swain had the ability to adapt himself to both the finer and the slapstick type of comedy.

220

The Gold Rush, (United Artists, 1925).
This film was one of Charlie Chaplin's greatest. His genius in developing comedy from gold-crazed miners and Arctic hardships, including actual starvation, created one of the finest of a long line of Chaplin films. Mack Swain gave an inspired performance, and his characterization in this film is considered to be his greatest work.

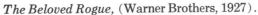

The Beloved Rogue, (Warner Brothers, 1927).
John Barrymore had been brought from the New York Theater to Hollywood by Warner Brothers. This film was based on the life of Francois Villon, the immortal French poet. Slim Summerville and Mack Swain were placed under contract by Warner Brothers to play the parts as Villon's cronies. There was a gay abandon and camaraderie in this great misfit company of thieves, pickpockets and their ilk who infested the sewers of Paris.

The Cohens And Kellys In Atlantic City,
(Universal, 1929).
Mack Swain and George Sidney had teamed up in a picture called *The Cohens And The Kellys.* This comedy was big box-office success, and as a result, they were teamed up again by carrying the locale to Atlantic City. The tried and true old cliche of attempting to mix the Jewish and the Irish after witnessing the theatrical bonanza of all time, *Abie's Irish Rose,* was very successful for George Sidney and Mack Swain.

ROLAND YOUNG

Born: November 11, 1887, London, England. Died: 1953. Height: 5′ 6″. Weight: 140 lbs. Dark hair and blue eyes. Educated at Sherborne, Dorset, University College, London, England.

He had traveled extensively throughout Europe and America. He also had a very fine theatrical background of nineteen years' stage experience.

His motion picture credits include: *Unholy Night, The Bishop Murder Case, Her Private Life, Wise Girls, Madame Satan, The Prodigal, New Moon, Annabelle's Affairs, A Woman Commands,* among others.

One of his greatest successes was his role of "Topper," the comedy series for Hal Roach Studios, and he also contributed to the smash success of *Ruggles Of Red Gap,* that great Paramount picture.

His typical style of the underplayed English humor went over in a big way with American audiences, and in his successful bid for permanent remembrance, the "Topper" series places him in the ranks of our greatest screen immortals.

ROLAND YOUNG

Here Is My Heart, (Paramount, 1934).
Bing Crosby and Kitty Carlisle starred in this film with Roland Young. Alison Skipworth and Reginald Owen played the supporting roles. His screen career covered a span of about thirty years.

Ruggles Of Red Gap, (Paramount, 1935).
Charles Laughton played the part of an English butler who goes to work for Charles Ruggles and Mary Boland, a wealthy Western couple. Roland Young and Leila Hyams played the supporting roles, and this company of distinguished players created a masterpiece. This role endeared Charles Laughton forevermore to the great American audience.

Ali Baba Goes To Town,
(Fox, 1937).
Eddie Cantor and Gypsy Rose Lee
played the starring roles with Tony
Martin, June Lang. Roland Young
also participated in this fantasy-
satire of politics in the 1930's. In this
scene Roland Young played the part
of a great Oriental potentate highly
enamored of June Lang's obvious
attractions.

The Young In Heart, (United Artists, 1938).
This story was based on The Saturday Evening Post serial *The Gay Banditti* by
I. A. R. Wylie. A distinguished cast included Paulette Goddard, Minnie Dupree,
Henry Stephenson, Janet Gaynor, Douglas Fairbanks, Jr., Billie Burke and Roland
Young.

Topper Takes A Trip,
(Hal Roach, 1939).
Roland Young had preceded this picture with one titled "Topper" which
was the initial picture of this particular series. The plot was based on a
ghost returned from the dead with
the ghost characters carrying out the
comic situations. Roland Young was
ably assisted by Billie Burke and
Constance Bennett.

223

CONSTANCE BENNETT

Born: October 22, 1905, in New York. Died: 1965. July 25, Walston Army Hospital, Fort Dix, N. J. Weight: 100 lbs.

Constance Bennett was the eldest of three daughters born to actor Richard Bennett and his actress wife, Adrianne Morrison. She was educated in private schools and at Mme. Balson's Finishing School in Paris. Just when it appeared that she was on her way to becoming a society matron she met Samuel Goldwyn who persuaded her to take a screen test. By 1925 she had played several major roles. In addition she played several stage roles, among them: Noel Coward's *Easy Virtue*, 1939 and a highly successful tour playing "Auntie Mame" in 1958.

Her most successful films included: *Sally, Irene and Mary; This Thing Called Love; The Goose Hangs High*, and *Three Faces East*. After a long absence from the screen, she returned in 1965 to star with Lana Turner in a remake of *Madame X*.

Her varied life included several successful business ventures in cosmetics and real estate, a total of 47 films, five husbands and several newsworthy court battles. She was best known for her brittle, sophisticated roles.

CONSTANCE BENNETT

Constance Bennett stars in the role of "Carla" opposite Gilbert Roland (to whom she was once married) in this scene from *The Woman Spy* for R.K.O.-Radio Pictures.

Topper, (Hal Roach-M.G.M.).
One of her most memorable roles was that of the ghost in this highly successful picture.

In 1931, Constance Bennett starred with Joel McCrea in *The Common Law*.

224